EAST OF LUDGATE HILL

by Arnold Ridley

Copyright © 1950 by Samuel French Ltd
All Rights Reserved

EAST OF LUDGATE HILL is fully protected under the copyright laws of the British Commonwealth, including Canada, the United States of America, and all other countries of the Copyright Union. All rights, including professional and amateur stage productions, recitation, lecturing, public reading, motion picture, radio broadcasting, television, online/digital production, and the rights of translation into foreign languages are strictly reserved.

ISBN 978-0-573-00012-6

concordtheatricals.co.uk
concordtheatricals.com

FOR AMATEUR PRODUCTION ENQUIRIES

UNITED KINGDOM AND WORLD
EXCLUDING NORTH AMERICA
licensing@concordtheatricals.co.uk
020-7054-7298

Each title is subject to availability from Concord Theatricals, depending upon country of performance.

CAUTION: Professional and amateur producers are hereby warned that *EAST OF LUDGATE HILL* is subject to a licensing fee. The purchase, renting, lending or use of this book does not constitute a licence to perform this title(s), which licence must be obtained from the appropriate agent prior to any performance. Performance of this title(s) without a licence is a violation of copyright law and may subject the producer and/or presenter of such performances to penalties. Both amateurs and professionals considering a production are strongly advised to apply to the appropriate agent before starting rehearsals, advertising, or booking a theatre. A licensing fee must be paid whether the title is presented for charity or gain and whether or not admission is charged.

This work is published by Samuel French, an imprint of Concord Theatricals Ltd.

The Professional Rights in this play are controlled by Eric Glass Ltd, 25 Ladbroke Cresent, London W11 1PS..

No one shall make any changes in this title for the purpose of production. No part of this book may be reproduced, stored in a retrieval system, scanned, uploaded, or transmitted in any form, by any means, now known or yet to be invented, including mechanical, electronic, digital, photocopying, recording, videotaping, or otherwise, without the prior written permission of the publisher. No one shall share this title, or part of this title, to any social media or file hosting websites.

The moral right of Arnold Ridley to be identified as author of this work has been asserted in accordance with Section 77 of the Copyright, Designs and Patents Act 1988.

USE OF COPYRIGHTED MUSIC

A licence issued by Concord Theatricals to perform this play does not include permission to use the incidental music specified in this publication. In the United Kingdom: Where the place of performance is already licensed by the PERFORMING RIGHT SOCIETY (PRS) a return of the music used must be made to them. If the place of performance is not so licensed then application should be made to PRS for Music (www.prsformusic.com). A separate and additional licence from PHONOGRAPHIC PERFORMANCE LTD (www.ppluk.com) may be needed whenever commercial recordings are used. Outside the United Kingdom: Please contact the appropriate music licensing authority in your territory for the rights to any incidental music.

USE OF COPYRIGHTED THIRD-PARTY MATERIALS

Licensees are solely responsible for obtaining formal written permission from copyright owners to use copyrighted third-party materials (e.g., artworks, logos) in the performance of this play and are strongly cautioned to do so. If no such permission is obtained by the licensee, then the licensee must use only original materials that the licensee owns and controls. Licensees are solely responsible and liable for clearances of all third-party copyrighted materials, and shall indemnify the copyright owners of the play(s) and their licensing agent, Concord Theatricals Ltd., against any costs, expenses, losses and liabilities arising from the use of such copyrighted third-party materials by licensees.

IMPORTANT BILLING AND CREDIT REQUIREMENTS

If you have obtained performance rights to this title, please refer to your licensing agreement for important billing and credit requirements.

EAST OF LUDGATE HILL

Produced at the Gateway Theatre, London, on April 11th, 1950.
Produced by Vivian Hall, the cast was as follows:

(In the order of their appearance)

MRS MALTRAVERS . . . . Hilda Barry
MINNIE HAZEL . . . . Cynthia Payne
BOBBIE DRUCE . . . . Michael Seavers
NORAH APPLIN . . . . Mary Savage
HARRY HEMMINGS . . . . Frederick Keen
HERBERT BEESLEY . . . . C. Denier Warren
JULIAN ELY . . . . Peter Rendall
ROBERT MCINTYRE . . . . Philip King
ALICE BEESLEY . . . . Carleen Lord
RUPERT BEESLEY . . . . Simon Blatchley
PAMELA BLANDE . . . . Veronica Nugent
A LATE ARRIVAL . . . . Anthony Pendrell

CHARACTERS

MRS MALTRAVERS – the charwoman
MINNIE HAZEL – a junior clerk
BOBBIE DRUCE – a clerk from another firm
NORAH APPLIN – the typist-secretary
HARRY HEMMINGS – a clerk
HERBERT BEESLEY – the managing clerk
JULIAN ELY – a clerk
ROBERT MCINTYRE – the senior partner
ALICE BEESLEY – Beesley's wife
RUPERT BEESLEY – Beesley's son
PAMELA BLANDE – wife of the junior partner
A LATE ARRIVAL – male

SETTING

At the offices of McIntyre and Blande, somewhere East of Ludgate Hill

TIME

The action of the play passes during one day in April

ACT ONE   Morning.
ACT TWO   Lunchtime.
ACT THREE   Afternoon.

ACT ONE

(Scene: The offices of McIntyre and Blande who carry on a business (purposely left somewhat vague) somewhere in the City of London, East of Ludgate Hill.)

*(The set is a divided one. The small section is right, and constitutes **ROBERT MCINTYRE**'s private office. There is a door to this up right centre and the wall below it is to be imagined. This office contains a large desk right with a chair above it. A filing cabinet, with a hat stand right of it, stands against the back wall. There is a chair for visitors below the desk, and a large safe, partly let into the wall, stands down right. The larger part of the set constitutes the general office. There is a large door up centre opening on to a corridor which leads to the other offices, cloakrooms, and stairs to the street. A large, semi-transparent window fills the backstage wall. The shadows of people approaching the office are dimly seen as they pass behind the window. A window in the wall left overlooks the street. A large office table or desk occupies the stage left centre. In the normal course of business, **BEESLEY** sits right of the desk, **NORAH** above it, and **HEMMINGS** left of it. A desk for **ELY** stands down left. There is a cupboard up left and a small table right centre, indicates the position of the wall presumed to separate the two offices. A desk, on which there is a small*

telephone switchboard, stands up centre facing right. This is used by **MINNIE**. *There are six hat and coat pegs on the wall right of the door centre. Five chairs for the staff and one for visitors, down centre, completes the furniture.)*

(See the set diagram at the end of the play.)

(When the curtain rises, it is about nine a.m. on a sunny April morning. The outer office is empty, but the sound of traffic can be heard through the open window left. In the inner office, **MRS MALTRAVERS** *is seated in the chair below the desk, fast asleep. She is a stoutish charwoman of uncertain age, wearing dingy clothes, a piece of sacking as an apron, and a hat ornate with fruit and flowers. By her side is a dustpan and brush, and a large mop leans against the desk. On her ample lap, there is a duster. After a few moments, two figures appear dimly outlined against the frosted window at the back of the outer office.* **MRS MALTRAVERS** *half wakes, shifts uneasily, snorts and relapses into slumber again. The door up centre is opened and* **MINNIE HAZEL** *peeps in.)*

MINNIE. *(Speaking over her shoulder.)* It's all right. Come in.

(She enters, followed by **BOBBIE DRUCE**. **MINNIE** *is a pretty girl of the junior typist class, aged about twenty. She wears neat clothes and carries a small cardboard attaché-case.* **BOBBIE** *is about the same age and is a wholesome looking lad of the type one would expect to find in a Y.M.C.A. gymnasium rather than in the local dance hall.)*

BOBBIE. *(In a low voice.)* Nobody about? *(He moves centre.)*

MINNIE. Not a sausage. *(She shivers.)* Brrr! Old Travertrout has left the window open.

> *(**MINNIE** throws her case and handbag on to the desk up centre, crosses and closes the window left with a bang, shutting out the street noises and, at the same time, awaking **MRS MALTRAVERS** in the inner office. She then turns and moves in to **BOBBIE**.)*

BOBBIE. *(Holding out his arms to her.)* Darling.

MINNIE. Dearest.

> *(They embrace. **MRS MALTRAVERS** rises and moves into the outer office. She stands watching them a moment.)*

MRS MALTRAVERS. Nah then, *nah then.*

> *(**MINNIE** and **BOBBIE** break guiltily apart as **MRS MALTRAVERS** moves farther into the office.)*

MINNIE. *(Embarrassed.)* Why, Mrs Maltravers. You? I thought you'd gone an hour ago.

MRS MALTRAVERS. Oh, yer did, did yer? Well, I ain't. See? *(This admitting no possibility of contradiction, she continues.)* 'Cause why? I'll tell you in a word – pickled onions.

BOBBIE. *(Cheerfully.)* That's *two* words.

MRS MALTRAVERS. Mind you don't cut yourself, Mr Sharp. *(She dismisses the interruption and continues.)* Pickled onions and Welsh rabbits. Gives me wind.

MINNIE. Oh!

MRS MALTRAVERS. Something crool. Wind all night. Scarcely got a wink. Nor Mr Maltravers neither.

BOBBIE. No wonder there was a gale warning on the seven o'clock news.

MINNIE. *(Reproving him.)* Bobbie!

MRS MALTRAVERS. *(Ignoring the interruptions.)* Then I gets palpertations, sits down a minute in Mr McIntyre's room and drops off. *(She looks up at the clock.)* Cor! Is that the time?

MINNIE. Yes.

MRS MALTRAVERS. Too late for Mr Perkins's then. I've done it nah.

BOBBIE. You mean you *haven't* done it.

MRS MALTRAVERS. One of these days I'll *say* something to you. Anyway, wot are you doing up 'ere, Mr Frank Sinatra? Nice goings hon. What would Mr Beesley say if I told him, eh?

MINNIE. *(A little alarmed.)* But you wouldn't.

MRS MALTRAVERS. *(Enjoying her moment.)* 'E's told you abaht being up 'ere before. I 'eard 'im myself. "Yore place is dahnstairs in yer own office, and I won't 'ave you up 'ere a-wasting of Miss 'Azell's time." That's wot 'e said. "And the next time it 'appens, I shall tell your hemployer."

BOBBIE. Who cares about old Beesley? He's not the boss of our firm nor of this one neither.

MRS MALTRAVERS. Oh, well then. Now I will tell 'im and we'll see. Kissing at this time o'day.

MINNIE. No, Mrs Maltravers – please don't... Bobbie has a *right* to kiss me now. *(Rather shyly.)* We're – we're engaged.

MRS MALTRAVERS. Since when?

MINNIE. Since last night.

MRS MALTRAVERS. *(Suspiciously.)* Where's the ring?

MINNIE. There isn't one. Bobbie can't afford one.

BOBBIE. *(Protesting.)* Here, I say!

MINNIE. You know what we agreed last night. *(To* **MRS MALTRAVERS**.*)* And it isn't really necessary. We're going to get married almost at once.

MRS MALTRAVERS. You don't mean you're...

MINNIE. *(Interrupting sharply.)* No, I don't. *(She holds* **BOBBIE**'s *left arm.)* We love each other and we don't see the point of waiting. People wait and wait and then by the time they can *afford* to get married, they don't want to.

MRS MALTRAVERS. Sounds all right.

MINNIE. It *is* all right.

BOBBIE. Catch 'em young and treat 'em rough.

MRS MALTRAVERS. You let me catch you treating *her* rough – that's all. Where are you going to live?

MINNIE. That's all fixed. We've got the offer of two rooms next door to Mum's. We've both got a bit put by and we're going to get the furniture...

BOBBIE. On the never-never.

MINNIE. Hire purchase. Bobbie got a rise last week and Mr McIntyre promised me one in May. They say "two can live as cheaply as one".

MRS MALTRAVERS. *They say* a lot of things. Wot about when the kids come along?

MINNIE. *(Shyly.)* We've been into that, too. We shan't have any – at least – not till we can afford it.

MRS MALTRAVERS. That's what *you* think. But things *'appen*. It's easy enough. Easy as fallin' aht o'bed – *easier*.

MINNIE. *(Trying to change the subject.)* Well, be a dear and wish us luck.

MRS MALTRAVERS. Orl right. 'Spose there's no 'arm in 'oping. *(She moves into the inner office and starts to collect her mop and other impedimenta.)*

> *(The telephone in the outer office rings.* **MINNIE** *moves to her desk and lifts the receiver.)*

MINNIE. *(Speaking into the telephone.)* McIntyre and Blande... Hello... Yes... No, not yet... Or Mr McIntyre, either... no... Not till about ten, I shouldn't think... Can I take a message? ... *(She is surprised.)* Who? ... Oh, yes, of course I will... No, I won't forget... Thank you... 'Bye. *(She replaces the receiver.)*

> *(***MRS MALTRAVERS***, carrying her mop, dustpan, etc., moves into the outer office.)*

Who d'you think that was?

BOBBIE. Jean Simmonds.

MINNIE. *(Moving left centre.)* No, idiot. Mrs Blande.

MRS MALTRAVERS. Mr Blande's wife?

BOBBIE. Or his great-grandmother.

MINNIE. *(Ignoring his attempt at humour.)* Jolly queer.

BOBBIE. Why? I expect *you'll* ring *me* up after we're married. What's queer about it?

MINNIE. The way she spoke. Seemed no end upset about something.

MRS MALTRAVERS. What did she say?

MINNIE. Nothing much. Just wanted to know if he was here. I shouldn't have thought he'd left home by this time. Then asked for Mr McIntyre. She ought to know neither of them show up before ten. She wants him to ring her the moment he comes in.

BOBBIE. I still can't see anything queer.

MRS MALTRAVERS. Nor me for that matter.

MINNIE. You didn't speak to her. There's something U-P, you mark my words.

BOBBIE. There'll be something U-P downstairs if I don't get a move on. Push off, Mrs M.

MRS MALTRAVERS. What d'yer mean – push off?

BOBBIE. I want to kiss my fiancée farewell.

MRS MALTRAVERS. *(Turning to the door up centre.)* Gercher! You'll soon get tired of that.

>*(**MINNIE** and **BOBBIE** embrace. As they do so, **NORAH APPLIN** enters up centre. She is a quiet-looking girl of about twenty-eight, dressed in a neat tweed costume.)*

NORAH. Well! *(She moves to the desk centre and puts her handbag on it.)*

>*(**MINNIE** and **BOBBIE** break apart.)*

MRS MALTRAVERS. It's orl right, dearie. They've gone cuckoo. Going ter get spliced.

NORAH. *(Turning.)* What?

MINNIE. It's a secret really.

MRS MALTRAVERS. Secret my boot.

>*(She exits up centre.)*

NORAH. Is she fooling?

MINNIE. No.

NORAH. Well I never. Good luck, Minnie. *(She kisses her.)*

BOBBIE. What about me?

NORAH. You're getting a big boy now. Good luck.

BOBBIE. Thanks, Miss Applin. *(He looks up at the clock.)* Cripes! *(To **MINNIE**.)* I'll see you at lunch.

> *(He exits hurriedly up centre. **MINNIE** and **NORAH** remove their hats and coats and hang them on the pegs, right of the door up centre.)*

MINNIE. *(Moving to her desk.)* Good Lord, it's Tuesday.

NORAH. What of it?

MINNIE. *(Moving to the cupboard up left and opening it.)* Mr. Beesley's clean blotting-paper.

NORAH. *(Moving to her chair above the desk centre.)* Is it serious – about you and Bobbie Druce?

MINNIE. *(Forgetting all about the blotting-paper.)* Of course. *(She moves centre.)* We decided last night. We can pool our money and get along somehow. What's the good of waiting?

NORAH. *(In a tense voice.)* What indeed?

MINNIE. Anything the matter?

NORAH. Of course not. *(She suddenly collapses into her chair, leans her head on the desk and commences to sob.)*

MINNIE. *(Moving in right of **NORAH**.)* What is it? Are you ill?

NORAH. N-no. I'm – I'm all right.

MINNIE. Shall I get you a glass of water from the cloakroom?

NORAH. No. *(She sits up and takes a handkerchief from her bag.)* It's nothing – sorry.

MINNIE. But...

NORAH. *(Dabbing her eyes.)* I ought to be ashamed of myself really. Carrying on like this. I *ought* to be glad to see you happy. You're a nice kid, and he's a decent enough lad – as lads go.

MINNIE. Yes, but...

NORAH. I suppose it's seeing everybody else's life running smoothly that makes me such a fool.

MINNIE. *(Easing right centre; quietly.)* I think I understand.

NORAH. *(Taking her powder compact from her bag.)* No, you *don't*, Minnie. I hope you never will.

MINNIE. It's to do with Mr Milburn, isn't it?

NORAH. *(Startled.)* What did you say?

MINNIE. I said, "it's to do with George Milburn, isn't it?"

NORAH. *(Powdering her nose.)* What nonsense are you talking? *(Her manner suddenly changes and she continues almost in a whisper.)* You know?

MINNIE. Yes. Well, I've guessed. It's all right. I won't say a word.

NORAH. *(Replacing the compact in her bag.)* There's nothing to say. *(She pauses.)* How...? *(She breaks off.)*

MINNIE. I haven't been spying, Miss Applin – 'struth I haven't. *(She turns away.)* Yes, I suppose I have really. But I didn't mean to. I didn't *start* by spying.

NORAH. How much do you know? *(She rises.)* Tell me, Minnie – you must – it's important.

MINNIE. *(Turning.)* It was last September. Sometimes I go in the lunch hour to Betty's Tea Rooms, down

St Jude's passage. I was having a coffee and sitting by the window on the first floor when I saw you talking to a man. I shouldn't have taken much notice of it only it seemed such a strange place to meet anyone – in a churchyard – all amongst those old graves. The next day you were there with him again. Then the next and the day after that. I know it's no business of mine and I ought to be ashamed of myself, but I couldn't help being sort of interested. You would, wouldn't you?

NORAH. Go on.

MINNIE. What made me more curious was – well – you were both so kind of furtive, always standing behind the old monument thing and looking about all the time. And he always stayed on there a moment after you'd gone. Then… *(She hesitates.)*

NORAH. *(Moving down centre.)* Go on, Minnie.

MINNIE. You'll be angry.

NORAH. No I won't. Please.

MINNIE. Well, I know it was wrong of me – wrong and mean, too – but one day I followed him. He was leaving the churchyard just as I was coming out of Betty's. I walked behind him up the passage and then he turned down into Half-Mile Lane. He went into an office which had a plate on the door "George Milburn and Co.", and there was a man on the step who said, "Hello, George, I've been waiting to see you." That's how I know. Now you're angry.

NORAH. No. But… *(She hesitates.)*

MINNIE. I suppose he's married.

NORAH. You've found that out, too?

MINNIE. No. I sort of guessed. Meeting like that on… *(She breaks off.)*

NORAH. On the sly?

MINNIE. Well...

NORAH. *(Moving left.)* Yes, he's married all right.

MINNIE. *(Moving right of the desk centre.)* You love him?

NORAH. Yes – I suppose so. *(She turns. With determination.)* Yes, I do.

MINNIE. I'm sorry, Miss Applin.

NORAH. *(Crossing centre.)* Does anyone else know? I mean, have you told anyone?

MINNIE. No.

NORAH. Not even Bobbie?

MINNIE. No, I swear I haven't. You see – after I'd found out that day, I felt sort of rotten. I still do.

NORAH. *(Sitting in the chair down centre.)* That's all right, Minnie. Only it's not the kind of thing I want to get about.

MINNIE. You can trust me, Miss Applin.

NORAH. Thank you, Minnie.

MINNIE. *(Perching herself on the desk centre.)* I don't want to be nosey, but – well – why not tell me all about it? It does you good sometimes – to get things off your chest.

NORAH. You're right. But a kid like you wouldn't understand.

MINNIE. I'm not such a kid as all that. Does he love *you?*

NORAH. He *says* so. Yes, I think he does.

MINNIE. Then why doesn't he get a divorce?

NORAH. He says his wife would never agree.

MINNIE. Does she know – about you and him?

NORAH. Of course not.

MINNIE. Then how does *he* know she wouldn't divorce him?

NORAH. I suppose – I suppose he does.

MINNIE. Excuse me asking, but have you been away with him?

NORAH. Only once. A weekend at Ramsgate. It was horrible.

MINNIE. I thought you said you loved him?

NORAH. Yes, but – signing the hotel register and being frightened of meeting someone.

MINNIE. Then I should chuck him up. I mean to say – what good can come of it?

NORAH. I've thought that, too. But – I can't. Anyway, I've got to decide today.

MINNIE. Decide what?

NORAH. He's going away tonight on business. To a place called Dijon in France. He wants me to go, too.

MINNIE. That would mean leaving here – losing your job.

NORAH. I know. But when we come back, he says he'll find me something else. Something better. And a flat somewhere.

MINNIE. Are you going?

NORAH. I don't know.

MINNIE. Surely you know whether you're going off tonight or not?

NORAH. I've got my passport and packed my luggage.

MINNIE. Where is it?

NORAH. In the cloakroom at Victoria. The boat train goes at six-thirty and I'm to meet him under the clock at a quarter past – if I go. I've promised to ring him and let him know later in the day.

(There is a short pause.)

MINNIE. Do you know what *I* think?

NORAH. That I'm a fool.

MINNIE. Not exactly. But I think *he's* a rotter.

NORAH. *(Rising.)* He's not.

MINNIE. Well, I think so. And there's a lot like him.

NORAH. I read novelettes, too. But *he's* different.

MINNIE. Yes. They *all* are. I think he wants it both ways. He wants to keep his respectability and his home comforts, and you, too.

NORAH. He hasn't any home comforts. He's unhappy.

MINNIE. If he was really unhappy he'd clear out.

NORAH. I've told you. His wife wouldn't divorce him.

MINNIE. I wonder. Anyway, he'd want to make a clean, open breast of it. Not a *sneaky* thing like this. *(She stops suddenly.)* Sorry.

NORAH. It's all right.

MINNIE. *(Rising.)* I'm not a church-going sort of one, Miss Applin – I always wash my hair on Sunday mornings – but – well, what I mean is, that love means sacrifice. Look at me and Bobbie. He's going to knock off his cigarettes and his football pools, and I'm going to cut out those cream buns at Betty's. Now, *your* part of the sacrifice is clear enough. You're going to give up a good job here and your respectability and run the risk of being caught in Queer Street. What's *his* part of it?

NORAH. *(Crossing to her seat above the desk centre.)* It will cost him a bit. *(She sits.)*

MINNIE. Money, yes. But what's money if you've got it to spare? I doubt if you'd cost him more than picking up an occasional tart in Jermyn Street.

NORAH. *Minnie!*

MINNIE. There. I've been and gone and said too much, but – don't do it, Miss Applin. Anyway, wait a bit.

NORAH. You said yourself that waiting is no good.

MINNIE. Not if you know what you really want. But – do you?

NORAH. I'll think about it. I've a few hours yet.

MINNIE. Think *hard*, Miss Applin. Please. You see...

> (**HARRY HEMMINGS**, *the second clerk, enters up centre. He is about fifty, tall, dark, shabby and lugubrious. He wears a long black overcoat and a racy-looking cap.*)

HEMMINGS. Ha! *(He looks up at the clock.)* Nine twenty-eight. Beat him to it. *(He takes off his cap and overcoat and hangs them on the peg nearest the door.)*

MINNIE. Beat who?

HEMMINGS. Beesley. Punctual Percy. Said he'd report me next time I was late. *And* he would *too* – a man with no bowels.

MINNIE. Now, Mr Hemmings!

HEMMINGS. Of compassion, I mean. Where's Ely?

MINNIE. On holiday.

HEMMINGS. *(Crossing to his seat left of the desk centre.)* No, he's not – due back today.

MINNIE. Oh, I forgot.

HEMMINGS. Not that it makes much difference to me. When he's away I only do his work. When he's here I do his work and have to listen to him too.

MINNIE. Well, he was at Harrow.

HEMMINGS. Yes, and if his rich pa wants his young hopeful to start at the bottom, why not in his *own* firm? Why pick on us?

NORAH. I suppose he thought...

HEMMINGS. There's nobody would have enough pluck to kick his backside. Well, nobody has here either – except Beesley.

> *(There is the sound of a door shutting offstage.)*

MINNIE. Look out. Talk of angels. *(She moves quickly to her desk and sits.)*

HEMMINGS. Angels, my foot. *(He sits quickly in his chair.)*

> *(**HERBERT BEESLEY** enters up centre. He is a short whipper snapper of a man aged about fifty-five. He has a pale face, wears a straggling greyish moustache and gold pince-nez glasses suspended from a cord. His manner is one of extreme alertness and pomposity. His voice is petulant and harsh, and he talks in short clipped sentences. He wears shabby but correct city clothes and carries an umbrella and a small brief case.)*

BEESLEY. *(Glancing quickly round the office.)* Mornin'. Where's Ely? *(He stands his umbrella in the corner.)*

MINNIE. Not here yet, Mr Beesley.

BEESLEY. *(Clicking his tongue.)* Tut! Tut! Mornin' Hemmings. Hum! Wonders will never cease. *(He moves* *right of the desk centre and puts down his briefcase.)* Don't suppose it will *last*. Mornin, Miss Applin.

NORAH. Good morning, Mr Beesley.

BEESLEY. *(Taking off his overcoat.)* I asked for three copies of that letter to Musgroves and you only did two.

NORAH. I'm sorry. I'll do another.

BEESLEY. *(Moving to the clothes pegs.)* Yes, waste of time, though – the *firm's* time. *(He surveys the pegs, then turns.)* Now, really Hemmings.

> *(**NORAH** and **MINNIE** busy themselves with papers, letters, etc., on their desks.)*

HEMMINGS. What's up?

BEESLEY. How many more times must I ask you not to hang your things on my peg?

HEMMINGS. Well, there's six of 'em – and all the same.

BEESLEY. That's not the point. *I* am the senior in the office, and I demand the peg nearest the door. I've had that peg since Tanner retired. *(He transfers **HEMMINGS**'s coat to another peg.)* This cap, too. *(He holds out **HEMMINGS**'s cap.)*

HEMMINGS. *(Annoyed.)* What's the matter with it? It's paid for.

BEESLEY. That's not the point. I don't consider a cap – especially a cap of such pattern – suitable city wear. It lowers the dignity of the firm. *(He hangs it on the peg farthest from his own.)* Coming in looking like a bookie's clerk. *(He hangs his own hat and coat on the peg nearest the door.)*

HEMMINGS. When the firm buy my clothes for me, I'll wear 'em.

BEESLEY. That is not the point.

HEMMINGS. Altho' a bowler doesn't suit me. *I* don't want to look like a rat.

BEESLEY. *(Moving right of the desk centre.) What* did you say?

HEMMINGS. *(Rising angrily.)* Why don't you pick on someone else for a change?

BEESLEY. Pick?

HEMMINGS. Yes – pick. If you can criticize *my* appearance, why can't I *yours?*

BEESLEY. *(Drawing himself up.)* Because...

HEMMINGS. *(Sweeping on.)* All right. I know the answer. Because you're the high-cockalorum and because I'm a junior at *my* age. And because I have a pint too many sometimes. And because I'm lucky to have a job at all. And because I'll never get another job if I lose this. And because you can get me fired and on the dole if you want to. And because both the bosses regard you as a tin angel – oh hell! *(He stops suddenly and sits again in his chair.)*

BEESLEY. *(A little taken aback by the outburst).* The 'bosses' as you choose to call them *do* certainly realize the gratitude they owe me for my long service with the firm. Thirty-two years of integrity and experience.

HEMMINGS. *(Wearily).* Oh yes, I know. Beg pardon.

BEESLEY. That is not the point. *Someone* must uphold the honour and dignity of McIntyre and Blande, and to submit to remarks such as yours, strikes at the foundations of discipline and efficiency. The next time...

HEMMINGS. I'll be thrown into the snow.

> *(**JULIAN ELY** enters quietly up centre and stands watching. He is about twenty-five years of age, and is wearing a smart sports*

jacket, flannels, a highly-coloured club tie, and a pork-pie hat. Normally he is high spirited, but this morning, he is depressed.)

BEESLEY. *(Drawing himself up for an oration.)* You really must realize, Hemmings, that…

ELY. All God's children's got shoes.

BEESLEY. *(Turning.)* So it's you?

> (**HEMMINGS** *busies himself with papers, letters, etc. on his desk.)*

ELY. *(Jerking his hat on to a peg.)* Who did you think it was – Donald Duck?

BEESLEY. *(Ignoring the remark.)* Do you know the time?

ELY. *(Simply.)* No.

BEESLEY. Nearly twenty to ten.

ELY. *(Lounging across to his desk down left.)* Fancy that now.

BEESLEY. There is no *fancy* about it. It is a fact.

ELY. *(Seating himself at his desk.)* Believe it or not.

BEESLEY. *(Becoming angry.)* You have been away on vacation – *with* pay – for a fortnight, and the very first morning you return – the very first, mark you – you arrive nine and three-quarter minutes later. I had hoped that, on return from your holiday…

ELY. I should enter like a ray of sunshine. Well, I haven't. I'm fed up.

BEESLEY. *You* fed up.

ELY. Yes, Comrade Slave. For two weeks I've sat in that Links Hotel in Scotland and watched the rain – only two rounds the whole time and the links under water. *Now* the sun is shining. I've a hangover headache; I've spent all my money; I'm 'in red' at the bank and me girl friend's run off with a sailor. So shut up.

BEESLEY. *(Scarcely believing his ears.)* What?

ELY. Shut up, Comrade Slave. Pick on old Hemmings if you must – he's got to listen to you – poor devil –

HEMMINGS. *(Looking up.)* Hoi!

ELY. *(Ignoring the interruption.)* – but I, *however*, if you get *me* sacked, you'll be doing me the best deed on earth. It would take the old man at least a month to plant me out somewhere else and I'd have a bit of golf in the sunshine. *(He idly turns over the papers on his desk.)*

BEESLEY. *(Realizing defeat, and breaking off the battle.)* Oh, well, if you've no integrity… *(He moves to his place right of the desk centre.)* Minnie. *(He turns to her.)* Isn't it Tuesday morning?

MINNIE. *(Rising.)* Yes, Mr Beesley.

BEESLEY. *(Indicating his desk, dramatically.)* No clean blotting paper.

MINNIE. *(Hurrying to the cupboard up left.)* Oh dear, I forgot. I thought I'd put it. *(She takes a sheet of clean blotting paper from the cupboard.)* I remember now. *(She moves right of the desk centre.)*

BEESLEY. That's not the point. *(He sits in his place right of the desk centre.)* To think is not enough.

MINNIE. *(Removing the old blotting paper and substituting the new.)* No. Mr Beesley. *(She crumples the old paper and drops it in the waste paper box.)*

BEESLEY. One must be sure.

MINNIE. Yes, Mr Beesley. *(She returns to her desk and sits.)*

ELY. Three bags, full, Mr Beesley.

BEESLEY. *(Ignoring* **ELY***'s remark.)* The same thing happened four weeks ago. *(He consults a memo pad in front of him.)* No, three weeks ago.

MINNIE. Did it, Mr Beesley?

BEESLEY. Here it is, in writing. *(He reads.)* "Minnie forgot blotting paper – *again.*"

MINNIE. Sorry, Mr Beesley.

BEESLEY. *(Setting off again.)* These minute details of office routine are not so unimportant as some of you imagine. They require discipline of mind, and discipline of mind is essential in business efficiency. Where should I be now if I had not concentrated on detail?

ELY. Where, indeed?

BEESLEY. I ignore your ill-timed facetiousness, Ely. Thirty-two years ago I joined this firm in the humblest capacity – junior clerk – little more than an office boy – my remuneration was eleven shillings a week. By diligence and attention to detail, I obtained, not only an increase in salary, but also promotion. I became third clerk, then second, Tanner retired – and look at me now.

ELY. Yes, my God! Look.

BEESLEY. I *invite* you to look. I hold a position of trust and authority. I have a wife and a son. I own my own house at Surbiton. I'm a sidesman at my local church, and next year I'm being elected to the presidency of the Mid-South Surrey Bowling Club.

ELY. Oh me, oh my!

BEESLEY. Not only that, but this very day, my boy is to enter a Public school.

ELY. Harrow? Which house?

BEESLEY. There are *other* schools besides Harrow, Ely.

ELY. Never heard of 'em. Which then?

BEESLEY. Dalrymple Academy.

ELY. For the sons of gentlemen.

BEESLEY. *(With sudden dignity.)* Yes, sir. For the sons of *gentlemen*.

ELY. *(Rebuked at last.)* Had me there, old cock. Sorry. I take it back.

BEESLEY. And I would have you know that...

*(**ROBERT MCINTYRE** enters up centre. He is an ordinary sort of man in the middle forties. Both he and his partner are the sons of the deceased founders of the firm. **MCINTYRE** is normally a cheery, nondescript fellow and wears neat but well-made professional clothes. His entry has a marked effect on **BEESLEY**, whose pomposity gives place to an alert obsequiousness.)*

(Rising.) Good *morning*, sir, *lovely* morning, sir. *(He backs a little right centre.)*

MCINTYRE. *(Moving centre.)* Good morning, Beesley. Good morning, Miss Applin. Morning all.

*(There are general polite murmurs from **MINNIE**, **ELY**, **HEMMINGS** and **NORAH**.)*

*(To **BEESLEY**.)* Mr Blande here yet?

BEESLEY. No, I don't *think* so, sir. Not unless he went straight to his office. Minnie, run along the corridor and see.

*(**MINNIE** rises and exits up centre.)*

It's only ten to ten, sir. You're on the early side yourself.

MCINTYRE. I arranged to meet Mr Blande at nine-thirty – important business. My train was late. I expect he's held up too. Damn!

(**MINNIE** *enters up centre and shakes her head.*)

Never mind. *(He turns to the door of the inner office.)*

MINNIE. Excuse me, sir.

BEESLEY. *(Officiously.)* Yes, yes, what is it?

(**MCINTYRE** *pauses, and turns.*)

MINNIE. Please sir, *Mrs* Blande rang up.

BEESLEY. When? When? You didn't tell me.

MINNIE. It was before you came, Mr Beesley. I forgot.

BEESLEY. Tut! Tut!

MCINTYRE. Well, Minnie?

MINNIE. She asked if Mr Blande had arrived, sir. I said "No", and she asked me to take a message. Would he ring directly he came in, or *you*, sir.

MCINTYE. That all?

MINNIE. Yes, sir.

BEESLEY. You should have remembered to tell me.

MCINTYRE. *(Mildly.)* I shouldn't have got the message any sooner, should I, Beesley?

BEESLEY. That is not the point, sir...

MCINTYRE. *(To* **MINNIE.***)* Get Mrs Blande on the phone for me, Minnie.

MINNIE. Yes, sir. *(She moves to her desk, lifts the telephone receiver and dials.)*

(**MCINTYRE** *moves into the inner office.* **BEESLEY** *follows him, fussily.*)

BEESLEY. Reakins haven't replied yet, sir.

MCINTYRE. *(Removing his hat and coat and hanging them on the hat stand up right; rather absently.)* Haven't they?

BEESLEY. Shall I give them a ring later, sir, and say...

MCINTYRE. Yes, do.

BEESLEY. What *shall* I say, sir?

MCINTYRE. *(Seating himself at his desk.)* That – oh, leave it for now, Beesley. I'll deal with it later. *(He starts to sort the letters on his desk.)*

BEESLEY. Anything *special*, sir?

MCINTYRE. Yes, I shall want you urgently later in the morning, so keep the decks clear. *(He looks at his watch.)* Damn Blande!

(**MINNIE** *replaces the receiver, turns and knocks on the door of the inner office.*)

Well?

MINNIE. *(Moving into the inner office.)* There's no reply, sir.

MCINTYRE. I thought you said Mrs Blande asked me to ring?

MINNIE. She did, sir, but there's no reply.

MCINTYRE. Oh, all right.

(**MINNIE** *returns to her desk in the outer office.*)

(He rises, gets his hat and puts it on.) I must go across to Craycrofts. Mustn't be late, either. When Mr Blande

comes in, ask him to join me there as quickly as possible. *(He moves into the outer office.)*

BEESLEY. *(Following **MCINTYRE** into the outer office.)* Yes, sir. Can I phone you there, sir, if there's anything urgent?

MCINTYRE. Yes, but there's not likely to be – not yet. Bye.

> *(He exits up centre. **BEESLEY** takes up a Napoleonic attitude in the centre of the office, makes sure that everyone is working, then sits at his desk and starts making some notes on his memo pad. There is a pause, then the telephone on **MINNIE**'s desk rings. She lifts the receiver.)*

MINNIE. *(Speaking into the telephone.)* McIntyre and Blande… no… don't mention it… sorry *you've* been troubled. *(She replaces the receiver. To **BEESLEY**.)* Wrong number.

BEESLEY. *(Conveying that **MINNIE** is in some way to blame.)*. Tut! Tut! Tut! *(He begins to sort some letters.)*

ELY. *(Turning in his chair, to **NORAH**.)* What's up with the Big White Chief?

NORAH. Who?

ELY. McIntyre.

BEESLEY. *(Looking up.) Mr* McIntyre – if you please.

ELY. All right. *Sir* McIntyre, *Duke* McIntyre, *Earl* McIntyre, if you like. Dammit, he was my old man's fag at school.

BEESLEY. That's not the point. The proper courtesies are strictly necessary for discipline and efficiency.

ELY. OK Comrade Slave.

BEESLEY. And *kindly* do not address me in that ridiculous manner. My name is Beesley – *Mr* Beesley.

ELY. Yes, sir.

*(***BEESLEY** *continues with his letters.)*

Three bags full.

*(***BEESLEY** *makes a gesture of annoyance.)*

But what is up with his lordship?

NORAH. In what way?

ELY. Seems a bit rattled about something. Didn't even ask me how I'd enjoyed my holiday.

HEMMINGS. Why *should* he? I didn't.

ELY. No, but you're a notorious sour puss. I sent him a picture postcard *too*.

MINNIE. *(Giggling.)* Yes. I saw it.

ELY. Good – wasn't it? "All my smacks go to the bottom." I'm surprised at *you*, Minnie.

BEESLEY. Will you *kindly* cease this silly chatter and attend to business.

ELY. *(Mocking him.)* Yes, sir. Certainly, sir. With the greatest alacrity, sir. *(He throws a document across to* **HEMMINGS**.*)* Here you are.

HEMMINGS. *(Examining the document.)* Dammit, this isn't *my* job.

ELY. Granted. But you'd do it so much better. I'm no good at sums – that was the term I had measles.

HEMMINGS. I'm up to my eyes as it is. *(He holds out the document.)* Do it yourself.

ELY. Come on. Be a pal. Buy you a pint if you do.

HEMMINGS. *(Grumbling.)* Oh, all right.

ELY. Thanks, chum.

BEESLEY. *(Rising.)* Once and for all – I will *not* allow this. The system of efficiency I have introduced into this office depends entirely on each member of the staff doing his own work. Hemmings, give those figures back to Ely at once.

HEMMINGS. Oh, all right. *(He throws the document across to **ELY**.)*

ELY. Pint off. *(To **BEESLEY**.)* How can you be so cru-el? Doing a comrade out of a stoup of wallop. *(He looks at the document.)* By the way, what *do* two and two make?

BEESLEY. *(Moving left centre below the desk centre.)* Now listen to me, Ely. For once and all, I will not permit...

(There is a knock at the door up centre.)

(He turns and calls testily.) Yes, yes. Come in.

*(The knock is repeated. **MINNIE** rises, moves to the door and opens it. **ALICE** and **RUPERT**, **BEESLEY**'s wife and son, enter. **ALICE** is a faded, neatly dressed woman of about forty-five. She was pretty once, but life in the suburbs has made her commonplace. She is a hesitant woman, and probably through long association with her husband, rarely finishes a sentence. **RUPERT** is about twelve, and like his father, wears spectacles. He is very timid and conscious of his new clothes.)*

ALICE. *(Nervously.)* Is Mr Beesley...?

BEESLEY. *(Surprised.)* Alice. What on earth...? *(He moves to her.)* Is anything the matter?

ALICE. No – not really – at least – I mean – not serious. I just wanted to speak to you.

*(**MINNIE** returns to her desk.)*

BEESLEY. Oh, well you – *(He hesitates.)* – you'd better come in here. *(He indicates the inner office.)* I'm sure… Yes. In here. *(He ushers her into the inner office.* **RUPERT** *follows.)* Have you wiped your boots, Rupert?

> *(***RUPERT*** nods.* **BEESLEY** *follows them in and closes the inner office door. There is general surprise in the outer office.)*

ELY. *(Rising and crossing to the inner office door.)* Of all the… *(He listens to what is being said in the inner office.)*

MINNIE. *Mrs* Beesley.

HEMMINGS. What a hat. And he was rude about my cap.

ELY. *(His ear pressed to the door.)* Ssh!

> *(Meanwhile* **BEESLEY** *has placed* **ALICE** *in the chair below* **MCINTYRE**'s *desk, and seated himself in the one behind it.* **RUPERT** *stands above the desk.)*

ALICE. *(Nervously.)* I hope it's all right – coming here like this – Rupert, take your cap off.

> *(***RUPERT*** takes off his cap.)*

BEESLEY. Tut! Tut! Yes, I should think so.

ALICE. *(Looking around.)* What a nice office. Is it yours?

BEESLEY. Well – I– er – hum – I share it with Mr McIntyre.

ALICE. Yes, of course. You told me. You know, I haven't been here since Mr Tanner retired.

> *(***ELY*** chokes back a laugh.)*

MINNIE. What is it?

ELY. Ssh!

BEESLEY. What is it, Alice? I'm rather busy this morning – er – Mr McIntyre may be back – you said you wanted to speak to me.

ALICE. Yes, dear – the tickets.

BEESLEY. What tickets?

ALICE. The railway tickets, dear – for Rupert and me – to Westbury.

BEESLEY. Yes, yes? I bought them myself yesterday. What's wrong with them?

ALICE. Nothing, dear. At least, I hope not. But I haven't got them.

BEESLEY. Where are they?

ALICE. You didn't give them to me.

BEESLEY. Of course I did.

ALICE. No, dear. I asked for them last night and you said you'd let me have them in the morning – you said I'd lose them. Then – this morning – I was upstairs finishing Rupert's packing – when I came down – you'd gone.

BEESLEY. But surely... *(He feels in his waistcoat pocket and produces two railway tickets.)* Oh, yes. Here they are. *(He hands them to **ALICE**.)* Very careless of you, my dear.

ALICE. But... *(She decides not to argue.)* Yes, dear.

BEESLEY. Your train's not till three forty-two.

ALICE. *(Putting the tickets in her handbag.)* No, but we were all ready, and it's so rarely I come up to town, I thought we might go and see Aunt Bessie at Notting Hill – it's quite close to Paddington – so I rang her – she said "come to dinner – lunch".

BEESLEY. Very well. But don't tie yourself up. You mustn't miss the train.

ALICE. No, dear – we won't.

>*(The telephone on **MINNIE**'s desk rings. She lifts the receiver. **BEESLEY** rises, crosses hurriedly to the inner office door and opens it, nearly knocking down **ELY**, who darts back just in time.)*

MINNIE. *(Into the telephone.)* McIntyre and Blande... yes, sir... no, sir... not yet, sir... yes, sir. *(She replaces the receiver.)*

BEESLEY. Yes? Yes?

MINNIE. Mr McIntyre, Mr Beesley. He wanted to know if Mr Blande had come in yet.

BEESLEY. *(Closing the inner office door.)* Oh.

ELY. *(Resuming his position with his ear to the inner office door.)* Narrow shave.

NORAH. You *shouldn't*, you know.

ELY. But it's so funny. Ssh!

ALICE. *(Rising.)* Well, I suppose we'd better...

BEESLEY. *(Motioning her back to her seat.)* One moment, dear.

>*(**ALICE** sits.)*

*(To **RUPERT**.)* You remember all I told you last night?

>*(**RUPERT** nods gloomily.)*

Well, as you're here, I'd better tell you again. You know how forgetful you are. *(He turns to **ALICE**.)* And you *too*, Alice. Don't forget to inform Mr Tadcaster that he's not to play football or cricket wearing his glasses.

(**RUPERT** *seems about to break his silence.*)

(*To* **RUPERT**.) I know you can't see without them, but that is not the point. It's costing a lot to send you to a high-class boarding school like Dalrymple Academy, and your strong lenses are very expensive. Also, the interval for repairs would interrupt your studies. One goes to school to work and not to play, so don't be led away by irresponsible comrades. Are you listening?

(**RUPERT** *nods.*)

Then stand still, my boy, and don't fidget. Concentration is what you need – and attention to detail. It's the small things of life that are important – clean books, use your penwiper, neat figures – order and system. It is to things like that I attribute my success in life. I started in a very humble way but by diligence and perseverance I've risen to my present position. I expect you to be a credit to me – *and* your family. Understand, my boy?

(**RUPERT** *nods.*)

And be sure not to forget the *other* things I told you – you know, when your mother was washing up the supper things – *Mens sana in corpore sano* – a clean body and a healthy mind. And don't forget to write regularly. I – er – your *mother* will want to hear how you're getting on. And be sure to call the masters "Sir". (*He moves to the inner office door and opens it.*)

(**ELY** *once more just escapes, moves to his desk and sits.*)

Now run along, my boy. (*He moves into the outer office.*)

(**RUPERT** *follows.*)

And don't put your head out of the carriage window or throw anything on to the line. (*He opens the door up centre.)* You can wait for your mother in the lobby – she won't be a moment.

> *(***RUPERT** *exits up centre.* **BEESLEY** *returns to the inner office.* **MINNIE** *takes a magazine out of her attaché case and starts to read it.)*

ALICE. *(Rising.)* What is it, dear?

BEESLEY. *(Strangely anxious.)* You think he'll be all right.

ALICE. Of course, dear. I bought the thickest under-vests and pants I could and...

BEESLEY. *(No longer pompous.)* This I think is the greatest moment of my life. *Our* lives. Rupert going to a high-class school. You think he'll do well?

ALICE. Yes, dear.

BEESLEY. He must. He must do well.

ALICE. *(Softly.)* He takes after you, dear. And look how well you've done.

BEESLEY. He must do better than that. That's why this chance is so important. *Much* better. *(With sudden bitterness.)* One bloody measly little clerk in the family is enough.

ALICE. *(Astonished.)* My dear, what do you mean?

BEESLEY. *(Recovering himself.)* Nothing, my dear – nothing.

ALICE. I've never heard you swear *before* – not in all these years.

BEESLEY. I beg your pardon, dear. *(He opens the door of the inner office and ushers her to the door up centre.)* You must be getting on. I've a lot to do. Give my regards to your sister and my love to Mr Tadcaster, I mean – you know. *(He opens the door up centre.)*

ALICE. Yes, dear. I ought to be home soon after eleven, and I've left your supper in...

BEESLEY. Yes, dear, yes.

> (**ALICE** *exits up centre.* **BEESLEY** *closes the door behind her and stands thinking a few moments.* **MINNIE** *puts her magazine down and resumes work.*)

ELY. *(Suddenly.)* Tripe and onions.

BEESLEY. What's that?

ELY. What's what?

BEESLEY. What did you say?

ELY. I said "tripe and onions".

BEESLEY. Why?

ELY. I don't know. I suppose something put it into my mind. It's as good a thing to say as anything else.

BEESLEY. Are you trying to be impertinent?

ELY. Not at all. What's impertinent about tripe and onions?

BEESLEY. You know perfectly well what I mean. *(He turns to* **MINNIE***'s desk, sees the magazine she has been reading, and picks it up.)* What's this?

MINNIE. Only a book, Mr Beesley.

BEESLEY. Books should be kept in their proper place – not in the office. *(He reads.)* "Clare's Paper." What twaddle. No wonder you make mistakes and forget blotting paper – wasting your mind on rubbish like this. *(He reads.)* 'Latest bridal dresses.' Bridal dresses. Anyone would think you were going to be married.

MINNIE. *(Off her guard.)* I am.

BEESLEY. What?

MINNIE. Only – it's a secret.

ELY. Well, I never did. You dark horse, Minnie. What *have* you been doing? Who's the guilty man?

BEESLEY. Be silent, Ely. *(To **MINNIE**.)* Are you serious?

MINNIE. Yes, Mr Beesley.

BEESLEY. Who is it?

MINNIE. Bobbie Druce – downstairs.

BEESLEY. Does he think he's in a position to support a wife?

ELY. You don't support wives these days, Comrade Slave, they support you.

BEESLEY. I was not addressing my remarks to *you*. *(To **MINNIE**.)* Well?

MINNIE. We're both going to go on working. Bobbie downstairs, and me here.

BEESLEY. And what will Mr. McIntyre and Mr Blande say?

MINNIE. I don't see that it would make any difference. *(Suddenly anxious.)* It won't, will it?

BEESLEY. *(Unable to resist his power complex.)* Well – I don't know. After all, you're careless enough as it is – that blotting paper for instance – we expect you to keep your mind on your work, not on... *(He breaks off for want of a word.)*

ELY. Don't say it, don't say it.

BEESLEY. *(Silencing him with a glance.)* Anyway, I'll speak to Mr McIntyre.

MINNIE. Thank you, Mr Beesley, but I *was* going to tell him myself later on. And ask him...

BEESLEY. Much better leave it to me, Minnie. Proper channels, you know – proper channels.

MINNIE. Yes, Mr. Beesley.

BEESLEY. *(Moving to his desk and sitting.)* Well, well, well. I don't know what's coming to you young people. *(With a feeble attempt at a joke.)* I don't suppose *you're* thinking of matrimony, Miss Applin?

NORAH. *(Angrily.)* No, I'm not. And if I was, it would be no business of yours.

ELY. Out spake brave Horatius!

BEESLEY. *(Taken aback.)* Really, Miss Applin!

NORAH. *(Recovering herself.)* I'm sorry. I've a headache. I beg your pardon, Mr Beesley.

BEESLEY. Granted. But – really...

ELY. *(Rising, crossing to* **MINNIE** *and holding out his hand.)* Gratters, Minnie.

MINNIE. *(Shaking hands.)* Thank you, Mr Ely.

ELY. And if you want to know the facts of life, just come to your uncle. I know them all and a few off the record.

BEESLEY. Get on with your work, Ely, and try not to be disgusting.

ELY. *(Moving to his desk and sitting.)* Yes, sir. No, sir. *(He pauses a moment, then adds with quiet meaning.)* "Mens sana in corpore sano."

> *(There is a pause while the implications of this dawn on* **BEESLEY**.*)*

BEESLEY. *(Rising and crossing slowly below the desk centre; to* **ELY**.*)* Mr Ely, I have come to the reluctant conclusion that you are a cad.

ELY. Reluctant?

BEESLEY. A cad, sir.

ELY. I know that, Comrade Slave, but the trouble is, I like it.

(**PAMELA BLANDE** *enters up centre. She is a well-dressed woman of about thirty-five, and reasonably good looking. At the moment she is extremely agitated.*)

BEESLEY. *(Turning and moving centre.)* Why, Mrs Blande! Good morning, good morning.

MRS BLANDE. *(Up centre.)* Is my husband here?

BEESLEY. No, not yet, Mrs Blande. We're expecting him any moment.

MRS BLANDE. Mr McIntyre?

BEESLEY. He's been in and gone out again.

MINNIE. I rang you, Mrs Blande, but there was no reply.

MRS BLANDE. I know. Where is Mr McIntyre?

BEESLEY. He's just gone across to Craycrofts. He left a message for Mr Blande to join him there.

MRS BLANDE. Get him on the telephone, will you? Ask him to come here at once.

BEESLEY. Certainly, Mrs Blande. *(To* **MINNIE**.*)* Get Mr McIntyre at Craycrofts.

MINNIE. Yes, sir. *(She lifts the telephone receiver and dials.)*

BEESLEY. *(Opening the door of the inner office.)* Perhaps you'll come in here and wait.

MRS BLANDE. *(Moving into the inner office.)* Thank you.

BEESLEY. *(Placing the chair below the desk for her.)* Is there anything the matter? Anything *I* can do, Mrs Blande?

MRS BLANDE. *(Sitting in the chair below the desk.)* No.

BEESLEY. Oh. *(He moves into the outer office, and addresses* **MINNIE**.*)* Well?

MINNIE. I think the number's engaged.

BEESLEY. Then try the other line – the other line.

MINNIE. Yes, Mr Beesley. *(She dials again.)* Hello... Craycrofts Limited? ... can Mr Beesley speak to Mr McIntyre please? ...what? ...oh, he has. *(To **BEESLEY**.)* Mr Mc Intyre has left, sir. *(Into the telephone.)* Hold on, please.

BEESLEY. Ask where he's gone.

MINNIE. *(Into the telephone.)* Are you there? ...can you tell me...?

> *(**MCINTYRE** enters up centre.)*

Oh, all right – he's here. Thank you. *(She replaces the receiver.)*

MCINTYRE. *(Rather irritably.)* Hasn't Mr Blande shown up yet?

BEESLEY. No, sir. We were just trying to get you, sir. *Mrs* Blande is here.

MCINTYRE. Where?

BEESLEY. In your office, sir.

MCINTYRE. Oh. *(He moves into the inner office, closes the door, takes off his hat and hangs it on the hat stand.)*

ELY. Something *is* up.

> *(**BEESLEY** sits at his desk, and during the following scene, the work of the firm in the outer office proceeds normally, but without distraction to what is going on in the inner office.)*

MCINTYRE. *(Moving and sitting at his desk.)* Why, hello, Pamela. Fancy seeing you. What's up with Arthur?

MRS BLANDE. I don't know.

MCINTYRE. I mean – he arranged to meet me early. Where the devil is he?

MRS BLANDE. I don't know.

MCINTYRE. What?

MRS BLANDE. I don't know. Thank God you've come. I'm worried to death. I … *(She bursts into tears.)*

MCINTYRE. Here, here. Steady on. What's the matter?

MRS BLANDE. *(Trying to control herself.)* I hoped he was here. I rang and he wasn't. And then I couldn't bear it any longer. I *had* to come up.

MCINTYRE. I don't follow you, Pamela.

MRS BLANDE. *(In tears again.)* I hoped he was here.

MCINTYRE. So he ought to be, but… what time did he leave?

MRS BLANDE. I don't know. I mean – he didn't – he hasn't been home.

MCINTYRE. *(Rising.)* What?

MRS BLANDE. He hasn't been home – all night.

MCINTYRE. Here, I say. Now steady on, Pamela. Everything's all right. Let's get this sorted out. *(He sits.)* Take it easy. When did you see him last?

MRS BLANDE. Yesterday morning, when he left to come here.

MCINTYRE. Perhaps he's ill. Or – an accident.

MRS BLANDE. I don't know. I'm nearly out of my mind. I've rung the police and all the hospitals, and all his friends and – everyone.

MCINTYRE. There's some simple explanation – there must be.

MRS BLANDE. What time did he leave here last night?

MCINTYRE. I can't say exactly, but it was fairly late. As a matter of fact, all the staff had gone. We stayed talking about a tricky little point that had cropped up during the day. Then, as luck would have it, a client came in. Funny old lady who lives in Suffolk. She'd brought up over twenty thousand pounds of Bearer Bonds – carrying them about in her bag as large as life – got them away from her bank with the idea of selling out and getting into some wildcat scheme or other.

MRS BLANDE. Was he quite well then? Quite normal?

MCINTYRE. Perfectly. After the old trout had cleared off – naturally we advised her to hold her horses – he was quite cheery – making jokes about her. I can even remember one of them.

MRS BLANDE. What?

MCINTYRE. Well, I asked him to lock the bonds up in the safe there. *(He indicates the safe down right.)* We gave her a receipt for them, so we're responsible. As he was doing so, he said: "By God, it's a funny world, isn't it? Look at this little lot – a fortune for someone. Have you ever considered the life we lead? The bus, the tram and the underground. A car for the weekend. A round of golf every Sunday morning, a few Saturdays at Lords and Twickenham, a month's holiday at Frinton or Bognor every year, and the rest of your life hum-drum respectable slavery."

MRS BLANDE. What a funny thing to say.

MCINTYRE. Well, it's true enough, and he was in one of his bantering moods. He went on I remember: "What a lark it would be to swipe these – all easily negotiable – and push off somewhere – South of France, Florida, or somewhere. Live like a lord. No more hum-drum, no more fogs, no more scrambles for the bus – why not, old boy?"

MRS BLANDE. And what happened then?

MCINTYRE. We had a good laugh. I locked the safe, and we went off.

MRS BLANDE. Together?

MCINTYRE. Yes. We had a whisky at the pub over the road and I left him waiting for a bus as I dived into the underground.

MRS BLANDE. And there was nothing unusual about him?

MCINTYRE. Nothing at all. *(He remembers.)* Except that he was carrying a bunch of flowers.

MRS BLANDE. A bunch of flowers?

MCINTYRE. Yes. Tulips they were, I think. He fetched them from his office as we went out. I thought they were for you.

MRS BLANDE. It's a long time since Arthur bought me any flowers.

MCINTYRE. *(A little awkwardly.)* Well, I'm a gay bachelor, you know. I don't know the drill for married men.

MRS. BLANDE. I wonder...

(There is a pause.)

MCINTYRE. What's on your mind?

MRS BLANDE. Nothing. I ... *(Suddenly.)* Do you think he's left me?

MCINTYRE. Left you?

*(***MRS BLANDE*** nods.)*

Rubbish, my dear. A stodgy old stager like Arthur. Absurd.

MRS BLANDE. It *does* happen, you know.

MCINTYRE. Yes. But not Arthur. Besides, you've been married for donkey's years. Ideally happy, too, I always thought.

MRS BLANDE. I suppose we've been about average. We've had our rows.

MCINTYRE. Who hasn't? Nothing serious – eh?

MRS BLANDE. Not till the other night.

MCINTYRE. *What* night?

MRS BLANDE. The night before last. I even forget how it all started, but he was irritable, and I felt rather rotten, and… – oh, I remember! – he wanted to see a film at our Odeon, and I wouldn't go. One thing led to another – I lost my temper and he said: "You get on my nerves. I'm fed up with you, fed up."

MCINTYRE. Just temper. We all say things like that.

MRS BLANDE. Arthur never has. Not to me.

MCINTYRE. Well, he has to *me*. Many times. I suppose it was all right in the morning?

MRS BLANDE. No, he was still annoyed. Anyway, we hardly spoke. You see *(She hesitates.)* – I locked my bedroom door and I expect… It was silly of me.

MCINTYRE. Now, look here, Pamela. You put such silly nonsense out of your mind.

MRS BLANDE. Suppose there's another woman.

MCINTYRE. Rot!

MRS BLANDE. The flowers, I mean. Suppose I've been living in a fool's paradise.

MCINTYRE. You'd have found out by now.

MRS BLANDE. I don't know. They say the wife is the last one to discover these things. Suppose he's left me for *her*. The row we had… *(She begins to cry again.)*

MCINTYRE. *(Rising and moving left of her.)* Look here, Pamela. You're letting your imagination play old Harry with you. You're tired out. You've had no sleep all night, I suppose –

(She shakes her head.)

– and your nerves are all over the shop. The old scout will walk in any moment now – he knows we've urgent business to do with Craycrofts regarding those securities. In he'll come and we'll all have a laugh and a drink. *(He takes her arm and assists her to rise.)* You pack off home, have a couple of aspirins or something, and try and have a rest – you need one. Leave the whole thing to me. I'll give him another half-hour and then, if he hasn't shown up, I'll get cracking. I'll try the police and the hospitals again, although I think it's a thousand to one he's all right. Come along now. *(He leads her to the door.)*

MRS BLANDE. I really feel I ought to wait.

MCINTYRE. No. It'll do no good. I'll get him to phone the moment he shows up, or I'll phone you myself. Be sensible.

MRS BLANDE. All right.

MCINTYRE. Now, dry your tears like a good girl. We don't want the staff to know about this, do we?

(She shakes her head and dabs her eyes with her handkerchief.)

Only cause a lot of chatter about nothing. *(He opens the door and ushers her into the outer office. With forced gaiety.)* So that's all right, eh? I'll give you a ring later.

BEESLEY. *(Rising.)* Good morning, Mrs Blande.

(She does not answer. **MCINTYRE** *and* **MRS BLANDE** *exit up centre.)*

ELY. The cut direct, Comrade Slave.

(**BEESLEY** *silences him with a glare.* **MCINTYRE** *re-enters up centre.*)

MCINTYRE. Get on to Craycrofts, Minnie, and tell them that matters must rest over till later in the day. Say I'll ring them.

(He moves into the inner office, closing the door in the face of **BEESLEY** *who was about to follow him.* **ELY** *laughs.* **MINNIE** *lifts the telephone receiver and dials a number.* **MCINTYRE** *paces the inner office deep in thought. It is obvious that he is a little worried.)*

MINNIE. *(Into the telephone.)* Is that Craycrofts? ... can I speak to Mr Craycroft? ...then will you take a message? ... Mr McIntyre says matters must –

BEESLEY. Rest over. *(He sits at his desk.)*

MINNIE. – rest over till later in the day.

BEESLEY. He'll ring Mr. Craycroft later.

MINNIE. *(Weary of interruption; to* **BEESLEY**.*)* Yes, Mr Beesley. *(Into the telephone.)* He'll ring Mr Craycroft later. *(She replaces the receiver, rises, moves to the inner office door, knocks and enters.)* Mr Craycroft is engaged, sir, but I left the message with his secretary.

MCINTYRE. *(Absently.)* Thank you, Minnie.

(**MINNIE** *moves into the outer office, closes the door behind her, and returns to her desk.)*

(He moves to his chair and is just about to sit when he is arrested by a sudden thought. For a second he pauses, then looks towards the safe. He takes a bunch of keys from his pocket, moves to the safe and is about to insert the key he has selected, when he notices something. He pulls the handle of the safe, and the door swings open.)

What the? ... *(He looks quickly at the lock, drops on his knees and searches wildly in the safe, throwing out various documents on to the floor. After a few moments, he rises, puts one hand to his head and clutches the desk with the other for support.)* Good God! *(He pulls himself together and moves hurriedly into the outer office.)* Get me a number, quickly. No, not you, Minnie. *You,* Beesley.

*(**BEESLEY** rises.)*

The rest of you, Miss Applin, Hemmings, Ely – get out.

*(Startled by his manner, **MINNIE**, **NORAH**, **HEMMINGS** and **ELY**, file out up centre.)*

BEESLEY. What is it, sir?

MCINTYRE. Don't stand asking silly questions. Get me the number.

BEESLEY. *What* number, sir?

MCINTYRE. Whitehall one-two-one-two.

BEESLEY. *(Moving to the telephone, then stopping and turning.)* But that's Scotland Yard, sir.

MCINTYRE. Of course it's Scotland Yard, you fool!

BEESLEY. But – whatever's happened, sir?

MCINTYRE. Nothing. We're *ruined*, that's all!

Quick Curtain

ACT TWO

(Scene: The same. Three hours later.)

*(When the curtain rises, the inner office is empty, the documents have been collected off the floor, and replaced in the safe, which is now closed. In the outer office **BEESLEY** is sitting in his chair facing right, and **MCINTYRE** is looking out of the window left. After a few moments, **MCINTYRE** turns, crosses and enters the inner office, turns, re-enters the outer office, and stands centre. He takes a cigarette-case and lighter from his pocket, extracts a cigarette and lights it. After taking one puff, he throws the cigarette down and treads on it.)*

BEESLEY. I can't believe it, sir – I really can't.

MCINTYRE. What's the use of saying that – over and over again? One can't deny facts, Beesley. What other explanation can there be? The safe is open, the bonds are gone and Blande has disappeared.

BEESLEY. I admit it looks bad, sir.

MCINTYRE. Bad. *(He lights another cigarette, crosses to the window left and looks out moodily.)*

BEESLEY. *(Rising, picking up the first cigarette and placing it in the ashtray on his desk.)* But, Mr Blande, sir. He's not the *sort* of man to indulge in an action like that.

MCINTYRE. *(Turning.)* What sort of man is any one of us? We think we know people thoroughly, but do we?

Take the office for instance. What do you *really* know of me? What do either of us know of Ely, or Hemmings, or Miss Applin or Minnie? We're locked up with them for hours at a stretch, we know their minutest habits, each little personal mannerism, but can we see inside their minds – know what they may be planning, or plotting or scheming? You've been here over thirty years, Beesley – in my father's time – before I ever took over. Yet, when it comes down to brass tacks, what do I know *of you?*

BEESLEY. I can assure you, sir, that *my* sense of loyalty to the firm...

MCINTYRE. Oh, don't be a fool. I'm generalizing, that's all. What I mean is, that it's futile to say Blande couldn't have done this, when it's perfectly obvious that he has.

BEESLEY. But I knew his father, sir, and...

MCINTYRE. *(Striding centre, left of* **BEESLEY**.*)* I don't care if you knew his Aunt Poppy. It stands out a mile. You heard what that man from Scotland Yard said, didn't you?

BEESLEY. Everybody makes mistakes, sir, even the police.

MCINTYRE. Well, they haven't made one here. For God's sake, man, how many more times must I go over the facts? First of all, Blande has a row with his wife. Then, by a stroke of bad luck, Mrs Winterstone brings in those bonds. He says what a chance it would be – to steal them and start life afresh – abroad.

BEESLEY. But surely, sir – he wouldn't have said a thing like that– not if he intended to do it.

MCINTYRE. I don't suppose he *did intend* to do so then. It was merely the thought running through his mind. Then – later on, probably the other woman had something to do with it.

BEESLEY. *What* other woman, sir?

MCINTYRE. That was Mrs Blande's first idea – before I'd ever found out about the safe – she thought there was another woman mixed up in it. Those flowers for one thing.

BEESLEY. Flowers, sir?

MCINTYRE. When I was leaving with Blande last night, he fetched a bunch of tulips from his office. He still had them when I left him waiting for his bus as I thought. God! I can see him now. The flowers in one hand, his brief case in the other, and his umbrella crooked over his arm.

BEESLEY. The flowers might have been for Mrs Blande, sir.

MCINTYRE. *Do* married men take flowers home to their wives?

BEESLEY. Of course they do, sir.

MCINTYRE. When did you last take some to Mrs Beesley?

BEESLEY. I – I don't remember, sir.

MCINTYRE. *(Turning and moving to the window left.)* There you are, you see.

BEESLEY. But there is this point, sir, and a most *important* point, too, as I see it. The lock of the safe had been tampered with – all those scratches and marks, and the lock itself out of order. Mr Blande had his own key – what was to prevent him from opening the safe in the normal way?

MCINTYRE. *(Turning.)* Well, you heard what that locksmith chap said.

BEESLEY. No, sir. I was answering the telephone.

MCINTYRE. Well, he said – *and* the detective agreed – that the lock *had* been opened in the normal way. It wasn't forced at all, but whoever did it, made the scratches and put the lock out of order *afterwards* – just as a cover-up.

BEESLEY. Yes, sir, but why…?

MCINTYRE. For heaven's sake, Beesley, don't keep saying why, why, why.

BEESLEY. Very good, sir.

MCINTYRE. *(Moving centre; with a change of manner.)* I'm sorry, Beesley, I don't mean to snap your head off. My nerves are all to bits.

BEESLEY. Not at all, sir. I quite understand, sir.

MCINTYRE. It's the *waiting* that's getting me down – not being able to do anything.

(The telephone rings.)

(He moves to answer the telephone, then stops.) You'd better.

BEESLEY. *(Moving quickly to the telephone, lifting the receiver and speaking into it.)* McIntyre and Blande… Yes… just a moment, please. *(He covers the mouthpiece with his hand.)* Mrs Blande, sir.

MCINTYRE. Tell her I'm out. Say that there's no news yet, but that – I'm doing all I can.

*(***BEESLEY*** nods.)*

BEESLEY. *(Into the telephone.)* Mr McIntyre's out, Mrs Blande… there's no news yet, but Mr McIntyre says – I mean he *said* he was doing all he could… yes, Mrs Blande… of course… the very moment, of course. *(He replaces the receiver.)* Don't you think, sir…

MCINTYRE. She ought to be told? What good will it do? I never see the point of the mad rush to spread bad news. Let her go on hoping as long as she can. After all, there *may* be a chance.

BEESLEY. That it's all right?

MCINTYRE. No, that the police may nab him. When Scotland Yard get busy they don't waste time. A description has gone out all over the country. Every exit port is being watched.

BEESLEY. Then he can't get abroad, sir?

MCINTYRE. Not too easily. But he's probably already *got*. Damn it all, he's had a good enough start. Assuming he came back just after I left him – well over twelve hours. There's a night service to the Continent – Dieppe, Dunkerque, and The Hook – to say nothing of flying. By now he could be in Paris, Berlin, Brussels, Amsterdam – anywhere.

BEESLEY. And the bonds?

MCINTYRE. Disposed of. You know as well as I do they're negotiable. As easy to deal with as currency notes – easier.

BEESLEY. And if they *are* gone?

MCINTYRE. I'm *responsible*. Blande is my partner. In the eyes of the law we're one. Besides that, I gave Mrs Winterstone my receipt. She gave them into *my* possession. Can I say: "Sorry, ma'am. That twenty thousand pounds of yours. I've lost it"?

BEESLEY. But what will you *do*, sir?

MCINTYRE. *(Dully.)* Go bust, of course.

BEESLEY. *(Suddenly stricken with fear.)* What, sir?

MCINTYRE. Go bust. Carey Street. File my petition.

BEESLEY. *(Hoarsely)*. Sir!

MCINTYRE. What else can I do? I haven't got twenty thousand pounds – nothing like it. I'll repay what I can, and then – well, the official receiver must sort it out.

Thank God I'm not married. I've only myself to think about.

BEESLEY. *(Hardly daring to ask.)* But – the firm, sir?

MCINTYRE. McIntyre and Blande? Done for, Beesley – napooh. A damn pretty end too. Perhaps Craycrofts will give me a billet. Funny to think about now, but we *were* talking of going in with them in rather a big way. Fat chance of that now. But old Craycroft may find me a desk somewhere. Hope to God he does. Sorry for you, too, old boy.

BEESLEY. *(Slowly.)* Do you really mean, sir – that – the firm is finished – these offices will have to close down?

MCINTYRE. Of course I do. What else *can* be done? I ask you.

> (**BEESLEY** *does not reply, but stares ahead with unseeing eyes.*)

The sooner the better – end of the week – today perhaps. Damn sorry for you, Beesley. After all these years – thirty, isn't it?

BEESLEY. *(Automatically.)* Thirty-two years and five months.

MCINTYRE. It's a long time, Beesley.

BEESLEY. Yes, sir. I remember your father engaging me.

MCINTYRE. You've been a damn loyal chap to the firm, old boy. I wish to God I could do something, but – you'll get something else. Better perhaps. You know your references will be all right, don't you?

BEESLEY. Thank you, sir. And the *others*, sir?

MCINTYRE. Who? Oh, you mean the other members of the staff?

BEESLEY. Hadn't they – better be informed?

MCINTYRE. Don't see the point of it yet, Beesley. Besides, you know what the Yard man said, "Keep the whole thing as quiet as possible while they're investigating."

BEESLEY. But is that fair, sir? In any case they must know there's something wrong – clearing them off the way you did, and telling them not to come back till after lunch.

MCINTYRE. I didn't want them here when the police came.

BEESLEY. No, sir. But suppose one of them got another offer? Hemmings, for instance. An offer of something else – this afternoon perhaps – and then turned it down. And then– well– what you said might happen– *did.*

MCINTYRE. Yes, I see your point, but...

BEESLEY. Then there's Ely and Miss Applin – and Minnie. Poor kid's going to get married.

MCINTYRE. Minnie? I didn't know.

BEESLEY. I was going to tell you, sir.

MCINTYRE. What a mess!

BEESLEY. Wouldn't it be fairer, sir, if you told them that something *was* wrong. Nothing definite of course, but just give them the hint.

MCINTYRE. All right. You can. Only for God's sake be discreet.

BEESLEY. Me tell them, sir?

MCINTYRE. Yes. In my present state of mind, I might easily say too much.

BEESLEY. As you wish, sir.

MCINTYRE. *(Taking out his cigarette-case, opening it, and seeing that it is empty.)* Have you got a cigarette, Beesley? *(He returns the case to his pocket.)*

BEESLEY. No, sir. I'm sorry, sir. I don't smoke.

MCINTYRE. Of course not. I forgot. Damn!

BEESLEY. Shall I run out and get some for you, sir?

MCINTYRE. *(Moving into the inner office.)* No, I'll go. A breath of air will do me good. This place is getting me down. *(He takes his hat from the hat stand and puts it on.)* Think I could do with a double Scotch, too. *(He moves into the outer office.)* You don't drink either, do you?

BEESLEY. No, sir. Well, sometimes a glass of ginger wine at Christmas.

MCINTYRE. *(Moving to the door up centre.)* Wise man. *(He turns.)* You'll sit tight on the phone, won't you?

BEESLEY. Of course, sir.

MCINTYRE. Right. Here – you've had no lunch. Shall I bring you in a sandwich?

BEESLEY. No, sir. It's very kind of you, but – I'm not hungry, sir.

MCINTYRE. Sure?

BEESLEY. Quite sure, sir.

MCINTYRE. Right, I shan't be long.

> *(He exits up centre* **BEESLEY** *moves to his chair, turns it, and sits at his desk for a few moments, with his head in his hands. Then he rises, moves to the telephone, lifts the receiver, and dials a number.)*

BEESLEY. *(Into the telephone.)* Hello… is that you, Bessie? … this is Herbert… yes, Herbert… quite well, Bessie, thank you, quite well. And you? Is Alice there? … I want to speak to her… yes, please. *(He closes his eyes and puts a hand to his head.)* Is that you, Alice? …listen, dear, listen very carefully. Something's happened, Alice. I can't tell you on the telephone... no, dear, I'm *quite* well... no, no, nothing of the sort... I can't tell you on the telephone, but it may – may alter our plans a little. I want you to come here at once... Yes, to the office... yes, of course, finish your lunch first... Rupert? No, don't bring Rupert. Leave him with Bessie – or perhaps it would be better if you sent him home... What train? ...Oh, yes... but that's the whole point... those are the plans we may have to alter – for the moment... no, not today at any rate... Alice, dear, I've told you I *can't* explain now... yes, come as soon as you can... Tadcaster? Oh, yes, of course... Yes, dear, and – don't worry, dear... Bye.

> *(He replaces the receiver, automatically takes some coppers from his pocket and places two pennies in a petty cashbox on* **NORAH**'*s desk. He then lifts the receiver and dials again. Into the telephone.)*

Telegrams? ... This is Ludgate four-three-seven-five... Are you ready? ... Telegram to Tadcaster T-A-D-C-A-S-T-E-R, Dalrymple Academy... R-Y-M-P-L-E, Westbury... yes... regret owing to – no – *through* unforeseen circumstances my son unable travel today as arranged letter follows. Signed, Beesley, B-double-E-S-L-E-Y ... yes... will you read it back, please? ... Thank you. *(He is about to replace the receiver when he remembers something.)* Oh, miss, how much is the wire, please? ... One and eight... Thank you.

> *(He replaces the receiver, takes some money from his pocket and puts one shilling and eightpence into the petty cashbox. He then moves to the window left and stands looking out, a picture of abject misery.)*
>
> *(***HEMMINGS** *enters up centre. His voice is a little thick. To say he was drunk would be an*

exaggeration, but the elongated lunch break has left its mark.)

HEMMINGS. May one return to the fold?

BEESLEY. *(Turning.)* Yes, Hemmings. Mr McIntyre has gone out.

HEMMINGS. *(Taking off his coat and cap and hanging them on the pegs.)* Then the private conclave is concluded? *(He is so pleased with this utterance, that he repeats it in a different form.)* The shecret shession ish shushpended. No, not so good. *(He takes a newspaper from his overcoat pocket.)*

BEESLEY. *(Still capable of annoyance in spite of his anxiety.)* It's easy to see where *you've* been.

HEMMINGS. *(Moving to his seat, left of the desk centre.)* To the local. And why not? "Return after lunch." That was my instruction. Although, in point of fact, I have not eaten – the appropriate time has passed, and – I have returned. *(He sits heavily.)*

BEESLEY. And in a fine state, too.

*(**BEESLEY** turns his back on **HEMMINGS** and looks out of the window.)*

HEMMINGS. I would have you know, my dear Beesley, that I am perfectly sober. I can read, mark, learn and inwardly digest. *(He opens the newspaper.)* Listen. Here is good news for the world's workers. "Unemployment figures show marked increase." *(He turns a page.)* And here, "The problem of the black-coated worker." *(He turns a page.)* And here again, an article, "Too old at forty." *(He looks around at **BEESLEY**.)* Makes you think, doesn't it? As I drank my humble pint and scanned these pages, for once, my dear Beesley, I found myself in agreement with your sentiments – we are indeed fortunate to have jobs at all.

BEESLEY. *(Turning; suddenly.)* You're not married, are you, Hemmings? *(He moves centre.)*

HEMMINGS. No. There was *once* a Mrs H.

BEESLEY. She died?

HEMMINGS. No. A slight domestic disturbance. And, as so often, alcohol, the root of the trouble.

BEESLEY. You mean – she drank?

HEMMINGS. No, she tried to stop me.

BEESLEY. Look here, Hemmings, I feel it's my duty to warn you...

HEMMINGS. I know, I know. Wine is a mocker. Strong drink is raging. Save your breath, my dear Beesley. I am a reformed character. What I have read in this journal has steadied me. I realize my peril.

BEESLEY. What I was *going* to say is, that there may be developments regarding the future of the firm.

HEMMINGS. I know. I *know.*

BEESLEY. What?

HEMMINGS. At yonder hostelry by chance I encountered a certain minion from the firm of Craycrofts. *(He wags a finger at* **BEESLEY**.*)* Ha! Ha!

BEESLEY. *(Puzzled.)* Craycrofts?

HEMMINGS. Oh, yes. The Ogpu is abroad. The Gestapo stalks the byways. The mighty Beesley is favoured with the words of kings, but the humble Hemmings gains equal wisdom from the murmurings of the multitude.

BEESLEY. *(Disturbed.)* Look here, Hemmings. Kindly don't play the fool. What exactly have you heard?

HEMMINGS. *(Again wagging his finger.)* Ha! Ha! What indeed. My lips are sealed.

BEESLEY. But...

> (**MCINTYRE** *enters up centre. He moves into the inner office, beckoning* **BEESLEY**, *who follows him in, and closes the door.*)

MCINTYRE. *(Taking off his hat and hanging it on the hat stand.)* I've been thinking over what you said, Beesley. You'd better tell the staff that there's a possibility of the firm closing down – in fact, *more* than a possibility. Only don't make anything sound definite, and be discreet. No word about Blande. You see?

BEESLEY. Yes, sir.

MCINTYRE. If you should want me, I'll be in his office. I'd better go through all his papers and see if there's anything we ought to know. *(He moves to the inner office door.)* You'll be discreet, won't you?

BEESLEY. Yes, sir. Certainly, sir.

> (**MCINTYRE** *moves into the outer office, then exits up centre.* **NORAH** *enters up centre.*)

NORAH. Is it all right now, Mr Beesley – to come back, I mean.

BEESLEY. Yes, Miss Applin. *(He looks at the clock.)* Where are the others?

NORAH. *(Taking off her hat and coat and hanging them on the pegs.)* Minnie will be here in a moment. I just passed her and Bobbie Druce. They were looking in a furniture shop.

HEMMINGS. *(Apropos of nothing.)* The age of youth is not the age of reason. The age of reason is not... *(He breaks off.)*

NORAH. What?

> (**HEMMINGS** *merely shrugs his shoulders.*)

(She exchanges glances with **BEESLEY**.*)* I see.

BEESLEY. When everyone is returned, I have to make a statement of some importance. *(Suddenly.)* You're looking very pale, Miss Applin.

NORAH. *(Surprised at his solicitude.)* Am I, Mr Beesley? *(She moves above the desk centre.)*

BEESLEY. You haven't heard anything, have you?

NORAH. *(On her guard.)* About what?

BEESLEY. About... *(He recovers himself.)* Oh, nothing. I merely thought you looked as if you were worried about something – some problem on your mind.

NORAH. *(Sharply.)* There's nothing, I assure you. *(She sits at her desk.)*

HEMMINGS. I know. I know.

NORAH. *(In sudden panic.)* What do you know?

HEMMINGS. The owl was a baker's daughter and all shall be revealed. *(He rises and strikes an attitude.)* I found not Cassio's kisses on her lips. What cared I if the whole camp – aye, pioneers and all, has tasted her sweet body, had I not known it.

*(***NORAH** *looks at* **BEESLEY** *for the expected outburst which does not come.)*

NORAH. Shut up, you drunken fool!

HEMMINGS. *(Sweetly.)* A fool, maybe, but not drunk. No, not drunk. *(He sits at his desk.)*

(There is a pause.)

BEESLEY. The point is this, Miss Applin. There comes a time in all our lives when we are faced with the unexpected – when we are forced to make decisions regarding... *(He breaks off.)*

NORAH. *(On edge.)* Yes, regarding what?

BEESLEY. No. We must wait for the others. My instructions are that the matter must be discussed by us all.

NORAH. *(Her anxiety mounting.)* But – Mr Beesley...

    *(**MINNIE** enters hurriedly up centre. She is rosy cheeked, happy and breathless.)*

MINNIE. *(Anxiously).* I'm not late, am I?

BEESLEY. Yes. But – oh, well, it doesn't matter.

    *(**MINNIE** and **NORAH** exchange surprised glances.)*

MINNIE. *(Taking off her hat and coat and hanging them on the pegs.)* I'm so sorry, Mr Beesley, but Bobbie was kept late, we had a lot to talk about and time flew by. *(She moves to her desk and sits.)* And, oh, Mr Beesley, you told me last night that directly after lunch I was to ring Hilton's and remind...

BEESLEY. No, leave it for the moment. There are matters of more importance than that – *private* matters.

    *(**ELY** enters up centre.)*

(Irritably.) Where is Ely?

ELY. *(Jerking his hat on to a peg.)* Ely is here.

BEESLEY. Of course, you *would* be last.

ELY. But not *least*, Comrade Slave. Not least, I trust. *(He moves to his desk down left.)* I was told to absent myself and I obeyed my instructions. *(He sits.)*

BEESLEY. Now, everybody – will you please listen to me with the closest attention. I have something to say.

ELY. *(In mock amazement.)* No.

BEESLEY. And let me say once and for all, that I shall permit of no interruption. This is a matter of the utmost gravity concerning everyone of us.

ELY. Ha! Ha! I told you something was U-P.

(**BEESLEY** *glares at him.*)

*(He meets **BEESLEY**'s glare.)* Sorry.

BEESLEY. I have had a long discussion with Mr McIntyre on this matter, and it has been decided that...

ELY. You're to be Queen of the May.

BEESLEY. *(Angrily.)* Once and for *all*, Mr Ely... *(His nerve suddenly cracks and his anger turns to pain.)* You are a heartless, selfish, despicable... *(He breaks off, almost in tears.)*

(Everyone is alarmed.)

NORAH. Mr Beesley!

BEESLEY. *(Struggling to recover himself.)* I'm sorry. I beg your pardons. You, too, Ely. *(He moves to his desk, sits and buries his head in his hands.)*

HEMMINGS. *(Rising slowly.)* Allow *me*. The noble Brutus is o'ercome. I will impart the news. Let Hemmings be the harbinger of good tidings.

BEESLEY. No, Hemmings. Mr McIntyre distinctly said that...

HEMMINGS. That the good news shall go from Ghent to Aix. I know *all* and allow me to speak. Messieurs, mesdames – M'sieur dam...

ELY. Translate.

HEMMINGS. *(Gravely.)* Ladies and gentlemen...

ELY. You mean gentlemen and ladies.

HEMMINGS. *(Bowing gravely.)* I stand corrected. Gentlemen and ladies. While we have been propelling our-purposeful pens; while we have been tabulating our tottering... *(He hesitates.)*

ELY. Tots.

HEMMINGS. Thank you, sir. While each of us has been performing his menial task, Time has moved on. The resolute historian of commercial history has been writing on the wall.

BEESLEY. *(Now somewhat recovered.)* For heaven's sake, Hemmings – sit down.

HEMMINGS. No, no, Beesley. For each man his moment. Ladies and gentlemen. *(He bows to **ELY**.)* Pardon – *Gentlemen and Ladies*. We have all known that events have been moving with a fleeting foot, and scarce an hour ago, even from the very lips of Pompey which all the time ran...

ELY. Blood.

HEMMINGS. *(Indignantly.)* No, sir. Beer. Beer. In other words, straight from the horse's mouth of one, Stebbins, who occupies a position of confidence at Craycrofts, did I hear the great news come by. The great and illustrious firm of McIntyre and Blande and their erstwhile yet friendly rivals, the house of Craycroft Limited – limited, mark you – are to amalgamate and together absorb such less fry as Perkins and Company, and Mason and Watson, to form in association a new combine to be known as McIntyre, Craycroft and Blande.

BEESLEY. *(Thoroughly roused.)* Once and for all, Hemmings...

HEMMINGS. *(Sweeping on.)* So do you see the reason for Mr Beesley's emotion. Thus was his story told. Strong men weep and millions rise to cheer. We hail the new era. Bonuses for Beesley, happiness for Hemmings, elegance for Ely, matrimony for Minnie, new hats for Norah – books in the running brooks and good in everything. *(He sways and sits down suddenly at his desk.)*

(There is a general chorus of excited chatter.)

ELY. Crikey, Harry.

NORAH. Is it really true?

MINNIE. Well, I never.

BEESLEY. *(Rising and almost shouting.)* Stop. Stop, I say.

(There is a sudden hush.)

NORAH. Then, isn't it true?

BEESLEY. No.

HEMMINGS. *(Rising.)* He lies – he lies i'the teeth.

BEESLEY. Sit down, Hemmings. You're drunk. If there was any point in it, I should go to Mr McIntyre and demand your instant dismissal. Only – *(Lamely.)* – there *isn't* any point.

NORAH. What do you mean?

BEESLEY. *(Moving right centre.)* It is perfectly true that the information Mr McIntyre did depute me to pass on to the members of the staff *does* concern the future of the firm. But it is information of an entirely different nature – entirely.

HEMMINGS. *(A little shaken.)* We shall see. *(He sits.)*

BEESLEY. Yes, Hemmings. When you are sober enough, you *will* see. What I have to tell you is this. Something has happened. Something of a very serious nature, and I am unable at present to give you the facts, but it comes to this – within a few days – a few *hours* even– the firm of McIntyre and Blande may have ceased to exist.

HEMMINGS. What did I say – amalgamation.

BEESLEY. No, Hemmings. The very reverse – ruin.

ELY. What?

BEESLEY. This is a most painful moment, but it is my duty to warn you, that each one of you, unless there is an unexpected development, will find himself and herself out of employment.

NORAH. Mr Beesley, you're joking.

MINNIE. *(Horrified.)* Mr Beesley.

BEESLEY. I wish to God I was joking, but I can assure you that I am speaking the truth. I discussed the situation at length with Mr McIntyre, and he agreed with me that you should be warned. For most of you, it will be a heavy blow. *(He pulls himself together.)* Naturally, my own case is different. I have been with the firm for thirty-two years, and the idea of parting must, perforce, arouse some feelings of sentiment. At the same time, of course, I have received many advantageous offers from other quarters, but I feel that my sense of loyalty to the firm necessitated their rejection. Now, of course, I am freed from such obligation. But for the rest of you – *(He glances at **HEMMINGS**.)* – for some of you in particular, I'm very sorry – very sorry indeed. That is all. *(He moves to his desk and sits.)*

(There is a pause.)

HEMMINGS. *(Raising his newspaper.)* Unemployment figures show marked increase.

NORAH. But, Mr Beesley, it can't be true. I can't believe it.

BEESLEY. It is true.

NORAH. Closing down immediately…

BEESLEY. Mind you, it's not absolutely definite – *yet*. Naturally, wages will be paid in lieu of notice.

(There is a pause.)

ELY. Well, I never *did. What* a stroke of luck!

HEMMINGS. Eh?

ELY. Nothing could be better. Here I am, out of work without ever being *sacked*. Nothing for the guv'nor to chew the fat about. In fact, *I'm* the aggrieved party. "Look what you've done to Sonny Boy, Poppa, dear. Pushed him into a wicked firm that's gone broke and thrown him out into the snow. Oh, Poppa, dear, *how* careless of you. How *very* careful you must be in future. Take *time,* Poppa dear, don't rush things. Bear this in mind and be very cautious." *(He leans back in his chair and roars with laughter.)*

BEESLEY. Really, Ely, I should have thought that even *you...*

ELY. I'm sorry, *Ex-*comrade Slave, but I really can't help it. I mean to say. Just back from my holidays, too. No hope of relaxation for another fifty weeks, and then – this.

*(**MINNIE** suddenly bursts into tears.)*

BEESLEY. There you are, you see!

ELY. *(Rising, full of contrition.)* I say, Minnie – sorry, old girl. *(He crosses to her.)* Oi, oi, oi! Steady on!

MINNIE. *(Sobbing.)* Go away, you beast. I hate you.

ELY. *(Genuinely sorry.)* No, no – don't say that. A bit tactless, I admit, but I wasn't thinking.

MINNIE. *(In a fury of grief.)* Then it's about bloody time you did. Just because you've been to a public school, and dress like something out of the *Tatler,* and just because you've a rich father and a decent home, and belong to the most expensive golf clubs, and are only made to *play* at work, you think this is funny.

ELY. *(Trying to calm her.)* No, no, Minnie.

MINNIE. Yes, you do. You over-dressed, over-fed cad! What do you care about any of us, so long as you get another holiday and can slack about hitting silly little white balls with sticks?

ELY. *(Protesting.)* Clubs, dear – clubs.

MINNIE. What does it matter to you that Mr Beesley has been with the firm thirty years and Mr Hemmings mightn't get another job because, as we all know, he drinks? And Miss Applin will have to go and hang round one of those lousy secretarial agencies, and I – I shan't be able to get married. Rotten selfish swine! *(She buries her face in her hands.)*

HEMMINGS. *(Rising and speaking slowly.)* I declare that speech well and truly spoken. *(He sits.)*

(There is a pause.)

ELY. *(Moving to his desk; quietly.)* Oddly enough, *I* do, too. *(He sits.)*

NORAH. *(Rising and moving to **MINNIE** to comfort her.)* Really, Mr Beesley, it doesn't seem possible that something like this could happen so suddenly. There must be some reason.

BEESLEY. Of *course* there is a reason, Miss Applin, *and* of course, as senior member of the firm I have been placed in full possession of the facts. I regret that I am unable to tell you more.

*(**MCINTYRE**, carrying some papers, enters up centre. **BEESLEY** rises.)*

MCINTYRE. Oh, Beesley, I ... *(He looks around the office.)* I see you've told them.

BEESLEY. Yes, sir.

MCINTYRE. *(Awkwardly.)* Well, people, I suppose there's no need for me to say how sorry I am. We're all pretty hard hit – myself included. Mind you, the position is not hopeless, but – well, things don't look too good. *(He pauses.)* In the circumstances, I don't see the point of you all sitting around here. You may as well push off. All except you, Beesley.

ELY. We'd rather stay, sir.

MCINTYRE. Just as you like. Well, go out and have a cup of tea somewhere – or something. Come back later on. *(To* **BEESLEY**.*)* Just a moment, will you?

BEESLEY. Certainly, sir.

*(***MCINTYRE** *and* **BEESLEY** *exit up centre.)*

HEMMINGS. *(Rising).* I know a bank where the wild thyme grows. *(He crosses up centre takes his hat and coat from the pegs, and puts them on.)* The problem of the black-coated worker.

(He exits up centre.)

NORAH. Are you better, Minnie?

MINNIE. Yes, I'm all right, Miss Applin. I'll be OK in a minute. Don't stop in for me.

NORAH. *(Returning to her desk.)* I'd rather. *(She sits.)*

*(***ELY** *rises, crosses up centre, takes his hat from the pegs and puts it on. He moves to the door up centre, then pauses.)*

ELY. I say, Minnie – I really *am* sorry.

MINNIE. It's all right, Mr Ely. I'm sorry, too. Speaking like that. I don't know what came over me. I was upset, see?

ELY. Forget it, Minnie.

MINNIE. Thank you, Mr Ely.

ELY. *You* forget it and I *won't*.

(He exits up centre. There is a pause, during which **MINNIE** *takes her powder compact from her handbag and powders her face.*

NORAH *rises, crosses to the window left and stands looking out.)*

MINNIE. *(Replacing the compact in her bag.)* I suppose I'd better tell Bobbie. *(She rises and moves right centre.)*

NORAH. I shouldn't. Wait till later. *(She turns, crosses to the telephone, lifts the receiver, dials, and speaks into the telephone.)* Milburn and Company? ...Is Mr Milburn in? ...

*(**MINNIE** turns and watches her tensely.)*

Can I speak to him, please? ...it's a private matter. He's expecting the call... all right... is that you, George? *(Her voice is low and tense.)* ... I told you I'd ring if... yes, I *have* decided... *yes*... yes, under the clock... yes. *(She replaces the receiver with an air of finality.)*

MINNIE. Miss Applin. You don't mean to say you're...? *(She breaks off.)*

NORAH. *(Moving centre; quietly.)* Yes.

MINNIE. But, Miss Applin I know it's no affair of mine, but I was sort of hoping that – well, after our chat this morning, you might think it over.

NORAH. I *have* thought it over, Minnie. But I've changed my mind again.

MINNIE. You mean...?

NORAH. This morning – after Mr McIntyre turned us out to graze, so to speak – I went down to the Embankment and looked at the river.

MINNIE. *(Frightened.)* Oh, Miss Applin. Surely you never thought of...?

NORAH. Drowning myself? Good gracious, no! But expanses of water have a strange clearing effect on the brain. I think a lot of our poets found that – Wordsworth, Tennyson, Shelley, Rupert Brooke.

I stayed there nearly an hour, and in the end I decided that probably what you said this morning was quite right.

MINNIE. *(Indicating the telephone.)* But you've just…

NORAH. Yes. Things have changed since then – circumstances, I mean – the firm closing down. It's the answer, isn't it? You said yourself this morning that if I went off with George, it would mean losing my job. Now, I've no job to lose.

MINNIE. But you'll get another. We'll *all* get other jobs. *(Anxiously.)* Won't we?

NORAH. In a way, I'm glad this has happened. I've always been a bad one at making up my mind. This has made it up for me. I think anything is better than answering advertisements again, and standing waiting on staircases, and being interviewed by fat men who stare at you as though they were trying to imagine what you look like without any clothes on. Anyway, it's settled now – once and for all.

(There is a short pause.)

MINNIE. D'you know, Miss Applin – I'm worried about it.

NORAH. *(Smiling.)* It's nice of you, Minnie, but don't. You've enough to worry about on your own account.

MINNIE. I dare say. But mine's a *simple* worry – if you know what I mean.

*(**BOBBIE DRUCE** enters up centre.)*

BOBBIE. *(Moving between **MINNIE** and **NORAH**.)* Here, what's all this?

MINNIE. *(Surprised.)* Why, Bobbie.

BOBBIE. I met that soak, Hemmings, coming out of the – cloakroom, and he said there was something wrong up here – to do with the firm.

NORAH. *(Moving to her desk and picking up her handbag).* I'll leave you to explain. *(She moves up centre and takes her hat and coat from the pegs.)*

MINNIE. No, Miss Applin, don't go.

NORAH. I was just going out, anyway. There are one or two things I want to buy.

> *(With her hat in her hand and her coat over her arm, she exits up centre.)*

BOBBIE. I say, Min – it's not true, is it? I mean, what Hemmings said. Your firm's not bust, is it?

MINNIE. Yes. At least – it's almost certain it is.

BOBBIE. But what – what's happened?

MINNIE. I don't know. Mr Beesley said we might finish up today.

BOBBIE. Beesley. *That* skate.

MINNIE. Then Mr McIntyre said very much the same thing.

BOBBIE. God! *(He sits in **BEESLEY**'s chair.)*

MINNIE. I'm sorry, Bobbie.

BOBBIE. It's not your fault, Min – but it does rather tear things – doesn't it?

MINNIE. I'll get something else.

BOBBIE. *(With forced gaiety.)* Of course you will. It's not so easy though. We've just got a new junior. The boss rang up the Labour Exchange. You ought to have seen the mob that came round. Jolly good lookers some of them, too.

MINNIE. *(Indignantly.)* Well?

BOBBIE. *(Hastily.)* Oh, not real class like you, Min, of course. But still...

MINNIE. I wish we hadn't told mum and dad now.

BOBBIE. About us?

MINNIE. Yes. You know what mum *is* – how she worries on about things. She'll say, "There you are. What did I tell you? Suppose it had happened *after* you were married?"

BOBBIE. I wish it *had. (Suddenly.)* Look here, *need* it make any difference?

MINNIE. We couldn't both live on *what you* get, Bobbie.

BOBBIE. I could sell that silver cup I got for boxing, and my gym medal.

MINNIE. And how long would that last? We shall have to wait, that's all.

BOBBIE. Suppose I joined the Army or the Air Force. You'd have an allowance then.

MINNIE. Yes, but I shouldn't have *you*.

BOBBIE. *(Rising and crossing to the window left.)* It's a bit of a snorter, I admit. *(He looks gloomily through the window.)*

MINNIE. We shall just have to wait.

BOBBIE. I suppose so.

MINNIE. You will, won't you?

BOBBIE. Will what?

MINNIE. Wait. You won't go and get hitched up with one of those good-looking ones downstairs – you know – what you were talking about?

BOBBIE. *(Turning.)* What do *you* think?

MINNIE. *(Softly.)* I *hope* you don't.

BOBBIE. *(Moving centre.)* You aren't half Miss Muggins, aren't you? Come here, kid.

>   (**MINNIE** *moves in to him.*)

(He puts his arms round her.) There won't never be nobody like you, Min. See?

>   (**MINNIE** *nods.*)

I'd wait twenty blinking years if need be.

MINNIE. Oh, Bobbie!

BOBBIE. Only I hope there won't be the need. Give us a kiss.

MINNIE. *(As they embrace.)* Oh, Bobbie, I *do* love you.

BOBBIE. Same here. Come on now. Dry those tears away. Everything's going to turn out OK. *(He kisses her again.)*

>   (**BEESLEY** *enters up centre. They break apart guiltily.*)

BEESLEY. And what's all *this,* may I ask?

BOBBIE. Lost your eyesight, old cock?

MINNIE. Bobbie.

BEESLEY. And what might you be doing up here? Wasting your employer's time, as usual.

BOBBIE. Oh, stow it. *(He moves to the door up centre.)* See you later, Min.

BEESLEY. One moment, please.

BOBBIE. *(Turning aggressively.)* Well?

BEESLEY. Come back.

>   (**BOBBIE** *moves down centre a pace or two.*)

I'd just like to say how sorry I am – for both of you. Very sorry indeed. That's all.

BOBBIE. Well, I'll be…

(He turns, truly amazed, and exits up centre.)

MINNIE. Thank you, Mr Beesley. *(She sits at her desk.)*

BEESLEY. *(Crossing to the window left.)* Don't mention it.

(There is a pause. **BEESLEY** *gazes moodily through the window.)*

MINNIE. Funny. I never thought of you like that.

BEESLEY. *(Turning.)* Like what?

MINNIE. Well – I don't hardly know how to put it – being sort of – human.

BEESLEY. *(Easing centre.)* Why not?

MINNIE. *(Unable to think of a reason.)* Well, I …

BEESLEY. A man can be efficient and methodical, and still have a heart, can't he?

MINNIE. Yes, I suppose so. *(Suddenly.)* Oh, Mr Beesley, you must excuse me for asking, but – I don't suppose there's any chance for me?

BEESLEY. What do you mean?

MINNIE. Where you're going. Your new position.

BEESLEY. *(Off his guard.)* What new position?

MINNIE. You know what you said. All those offers you've had – the ones you couldn't take – because of the firm.

BEESLEY. *(Hastily.)* Oh, yes, yes.

MINNIE. I *am* glad, for your sake, Mr Beesley. It would be awful for you after all these years, if you hadn't anything. *(Shyly.)* I don't suppose you could take me with you? I'd work hard and try to remember the blotting-paper on Tuesdays – really I would.

BEESLEY. Well, it may not be easy. It depends very much on which position I – er – decide to accept. The firm may be fully staffed as regards junior employees. But – er – I'll do my best.

MINNIE. Thanks, ever so.

BEESLEY. *(Hastily.)* But don't build on it. I mean – don't let it stop you looking around for yourself.

MINNIE. No, Mr Beesley.

(The telephone rings.)

(She lifts the receiver and speaks into it.) McIntyre and Blande... yes, hold on, please. *(To* **BEESLEY**.*)* It's Mrs Blande. (**BEESLEY** *moving to* **MINNIE***'s desk.)* I'll take it. *(He takes the receiver from her. Into the phone.)* Mr Beesley speaking... no, Mrs Blande, Mr McIntyre is still out... no, not yet... yes, of course I will, Mrs Blande... Bye. *(He replaces the receiver.)*

MINNIE. Mr Blande's got something to do with it, hasn't he?

BEESLEY. With what?

MINNIE. With what's happened. I thought when she rang first thing this morning, that there was something wrong.

BEESLEY. I can't tell you. Be a good girl and don't ask questions.

MINNIE. No, Mr Beesley.

(There is a knock at the door up centre.)

BEESLEY. Come in.

(**ALICE BEESLEY** *enters up centre. As usual, she is rather flustered.)*

Oh, here you are, Alice.

ALICE. Yes, dear. You *did* say the office, didn't you? I should have been here before, but I got on the wrong bus – I mean the bus going the wrong way. I didn't notice till I was nearly at Edgware.

BEESLEY. *(Impatiently).* Yes, yes, yes. Very careless of you, my dear. *(He turns to* **MINNIE**.*)* Just run and tell Mr McIntyre I'm engaged, will you? He's in Mr Blande's office. See if you can do anything. He may like a cup of tea.

MINNIE. *(Rising.)* Yes, Mr Beesley. *(She moves to the door up centre.)* Shall I make you one, too?

BEESLEY. *(Abstractedly.)* One what?

MINNIE. A cup of tea.

BEESLEY. No, no. Not now.

*(***MINNIE** *exits up centre.)*

ALICE. What is it, Herbert? You look so white. You said you weren't ill, but…

BEESLEY. I am *not* ill.

ALICE. But *something's* the matter.

BEESLEY. Yes, something is the matter. *(He indicates the chair down centre.)* You'd better sit down. *(He sits in his own chair right of the desk.)*

ALICE. *(Seating herself.)* Yes, dear. But I do wish you'd tell me…

BEESLEY. I'm *going* to tell you. *(Suddenly.)* Where's Rupert?

ALICE. You told me not to bring him. I've sent him home. You said I was to.

BEESLEY. Yes, yes, yes. Of course.

ALICE. I don't know what Mr Tadcaster will think – me not bringing Rupert after it was all arranged. Have you telegraphed him?

BEESLEY. Yes, yes, yes. *Please* don't interrupt.

ALICE. No, dear. But the new term opens tomorrow, and...

BEESLEY. The new term does *not* open tomorrow.

ALICE. But, dear, it *does*. The twenty-fourth. Mr Tadcaster distinctly said so.

BEESLEY. What I mean is, that it does not open for Rupert. We can't send him to Dalrymple Academy.

ALICE. But why not, dear? It's all arranged, and...

BEESLEY. Listen to me, Alice, *please*. I've lost my job.

ALICE. *(Unbelievingly.)* What?

BEESLEY. I say *I've lost my job.*

ALICE. Oh, Herbert. What *have* you done?

BEESLEY. *(Irritated.)* What have I done? Nothing, of course. Why, you don't think I've been *dismissed,* do you?

ALICE. But, dear, you said...

BEESLEY. I suppose what I should have said was, that my job no longer exists.

ALICE. I don't understand.

BEESLEY. Then, *listen,* Alice. Something very terrible has happened – McIntyre and Blande is finished. The firm is closing down. This week – tonight possibly.

ALICE. It *can't*!

BEESLEY. It can and it *will*. Mr Blande has defaulted. Run away with twenty thousand pounds worth of negotiable securities. There's another woman mixed up in it, so it would appear. Anyway, Mr McIntyre is ruined, the firm is closing down, and – I'm out of a job.

ALICE. I can't believe it.

BEESLEY. Nor could I at first. But it's true. I might not have told you yet, but I had to stop you from taking Rupert to Westbury.

ALICE. Oh, Herbert. *(Cheerfully.)* But you'll get something else.

BEESLEY. *(Flatly.)* Where?

ALICE. *(Vaguely.)* Why – anywhere.

(**BEESLEY** *laughs harshly.*)

I mean – with all your experience. You've been here over thirty years.

BEESLEY. Thirty-*two* years. But that doesn't count for much these days.

ALICE. It's a long time, dear.

BEESLEY. *(Rising). Too* long. *(He moves left centre, below the desk.)* This is the day of the young man – smart fellows like young Ely. I see now it's a mistake to stay all your life with one firm. You gain experience, of course, but only of *one* sort of work. You go on with old out-of-date methods, and you don't notice what's happening. Then – all of a sudden – you find yourself out of it.

ALICE. But anyone would be only too anxious to have *you*.

BEESLEY. Why should they be? I'm fifty-five, and I've suddenly realized that, as a commercial proposition, I'm a back number.

ALICE. Don't be silly, dear. You're nothing of the sort. Think of all those other offers.

BEESLEY. Eh?

ALICE. *(Rising.)* All the ones you've told me about. *(She moves in right of him.)* Why, this may be a blessing in disguise. Don't think I don't understand how you feel. It will be a wrench leaving here after so long, but you've said yourself time after time, that you ought to accept something else – at a higher salary – that it was only your loyalty to Mr McIntyre and Mr Blande that made you stay on here. Don't you see?

BEESLEY. Yes, I see –

ALICE. Well, dear...

BEESLEY. *(Turning and moving to the window left.)* – that I've been a fool and a liar.

ALICE. You, a liar. Never.

BEESLEY. *(Dully.)* There *haven't* been any other offers – ever.

ALICE. *(Moving to the chair down centre and sitting.)* But, dear – I distinctly remember you telling me that...

BEESLEY. *(Turning.)* I tell you there *haven't* been. Just my silly pride and conceit, I suppose. As a matter of fact, I had a narrow squeak *here* six months ago. Mr Blande suggested I might like to retire.

ALICE. *(Indignantly.)* How dare he?

BEESLEY. *(Moving centre.)* He said they might be prepared to give me a small pension – That they needed someone younger. But I spoke to Mr McIntyre about it, and they agreed that I should stay on – at a reduction.

ALICE. A reduction of salary. *(She pauses.)* But you never told me.

BEESLEY. No.

ALICE. And you've been giving me the same for housekeeping.

BEESLEY. I didn't tell you – I was ashamed.

ALICE. You don't drink, you don't smoke, and you don't gamble. *(Suddenly.)* You haven't been going without your proper lunches, have you?

BEESLEY. *(Evading the question.)* Don't be silly.

ALICE. I remember now – that day Rupert was knocked down by the bicycle – I rang you at the Dorset Restaurant, and they said you hadn't been there lately.

BEESLEY. I've been perfectly all right, and economy was essential – for the boy's sake.

ALICE. Oh, Herbert.

BEESLEY. I was determined he should go to Dalrymple Academy.

ALICE. *(Bursting into tears.)* Oh – my dear.

BEESLEY. *(Moving in left of her.)* Now, I've let you down. Let you *both* down. I agree, it's enough to make any woman cry.

ALICE. I'm not crying for myself – not even for Rupert. I'm crying for *you*. Because you never told me. There's that spare room. I could have taken a lodger.

BEESLEY. *(With a return of his old spirit.)* And have the neighbours know? Not likely.

ALICE. *(Taking his hand.)* Try not to worry, dear. Everything will be all right. We'll find a way out.

BEESLEY. *(Doubtfully.)* Yes, yes, of course.

(The telephone rings.)

(He moves to the telephone, lifts the receiver and speaks into it.) McIntyre and Blande... Mr McIntyre? ... what name, please? ... will you hold on, please. *(He switches over and rings the extension.)* Mr McIntyre, sir... There's a Mr Andrews on the line, sir... Yes, sir, I'll put him through. *(He switches the line through, replaces the receiver, and turns to* **ALICE**.*)* You'd better go home now, dear. Some of the others will be coming back.

ALICE. *(Rising.)* Yes, dear. Shall I tell Rupert?

BEESLEY. No. Leave it to me. I'll explain that we're going to send him to another school – a *better* school, later on. I'll arrange for him to go back to the Council school later in the week. Perhaps if I give him some extra coaching in the evenings, he may win a scholarship to the Secondary.

ALICE. I'm sure he'll try, dear.

BEESLEY. Try not to worry, dear. I'm sorry I've let you down.

ALICE. You haven't, Herbert – you haven't. You won't be late, will you?

BEESLEY. No, dear. I shan't be late. *(He ushers her to the door up centre.)* And there's still a hope, you know. They may catch Blande. The police, I mean.

ALICE. If they do, I hope they hang him.

> *(**ALICE** exits up centre. **BEESLEY** moves to the window left. After a few moments, **MCINTYRE**, looking very perturbed, enters quickly up centre. **BEESLEY** turns sharply.)*

BEESLEY. Sir?

MCINTYRE. Well, we know all about it *now*.

BEESLEY. *(Moving centre.) What,* sir?

MCINTYRE. The phone call you put through. It was that man from Scotland Yard.

BEESLEY. To do with Mr Blande. *(With a sudden hope.)* The police have caught him, sir?

MCINTYRE. *(Sitting in the chair down centre.)* No. He's *dead.*

BEESLEY. *What?*

MCINTYRE. He's dead, I tell you. They've just told me. A message from Folkestone. A detective there saw a man answering to his description and went up to question him. The man broke away and ran up the landing stage. There was a paddle boat just pulling out – an excursion steamer – and the man tried to jump aboard. He missed his footing and fell in between – into the paddle

BEESLEY. Killed?

MCINTYRE. Chopped to bits. Absolutely unrecognizable.

BEESLEY. Then how can we be sure…

MCINTYRE. Because of the brief case. It missed the wheel and they got it out. Blande's.

BEESLEY. Sir. And the securities?

MCINTYRE. Gone. Not a sign.

BEESLEY. *(Slowly.)* Good God!

MCINTYRE. So that's the finish of it.

*(The telephone rings. **BEESLEY** moves to it and lifts the receiver.)*

BEESLEY. *(Into the telephone.)* McIntyre and Blande…

*(He covers the receiver with his hand and turns to **MCINTYRE**.)*

Mrs Blande, sir.

MCINTYRE. Tell her that – no.

(He rises, moves with his hand outstretched for the receiver as – the curtain falls.)

ACT THREE

(Scene – The same. Two hours later.)

(When the curtain rises, **HEMMINGS** *is sitting at his desk, half asleep, and* **NORAH** *is standing above the desk centre, clearing up her papers and desk.* **MRS MALTRAVERS** *is sitting in the chair down centre. She is wearing her outdoor clothes. Dirty teacups are scattered around on the various desks. After a few moments,* **MINNIE** *enters up centre, carrying a cup of tea, which she gives to* **MRS MALTRAVERS**.*)*

MRS MALTRAVERS. *(Taking the cup of tea.)* Thank you, dearie. *And* I can do with it after a day like this one. *(She sips noisily.)* Mysteries is orl right so long as you don't get mixed up in 'em.

MINNIE. *(Perching herself on the corner of the desk centre.)* Well, *I* can't tell you any more. Mr McIntyre is out, Mr Beesley's out, and Mr Blande hasn't come in all day.

MRS MALTRAVERS. 'Twouldn't surprise me if it wasn't murder.

MINNIE. *(Astonished.)* Murder?

MRS MALTRAVERS. That's what I said.

HEMMINGS. *(Half waking.)* Murder most foul as at the best it is. But the most strange and unnatural. *(He dozes again.)*

MRS MALTRAVERS. What's the matter with 'im?

NORAH. Hang-over. He had an extra hour for lunch.

MRS MALTRAVERS. Ho, I see. *(She drinks.)*

MINNIE. But, Mrs Maltravers, I really can't see where you get the idea of murder from.

MRS MALTRAVERS. Ain't the police in on it?

MINNIE. Yes, but...

MRS MALTRAVERS. There you are, you see!

MINNIE. But the police are concerned with other things besides.

MRS MALTRAVERS. You can't tell me nothink about the police. My first 'usband was mixed up with the police all 'is life.

MINNIE. Oh?

MRS MALTRAVERS. Yers. 'E *died* in Wormwood Scrubs. *(She finishes her tea.)*

MINNIE. But you're the only one the police have asked questions from.

MRS MALTRAVERS. *(Passing her empty cup and saucer to* **MINNIE.***)* 'Cause why? Because I'm only a workin' woman.

> *(***MINNIE** *puts the cup and saucer on the desk centre.)*

That's the way of the world. If anythink goes wrong – take it out of the poor. *(She chuckles.)* But 'e didn't get much change aht o' me.

NORAH. Who?

MRS MALTRAVERS. Why, that police chap I was tellin' you abaht. There was I cookin' Mr Maltravers' dinner as calm as possible – nice bit offish it was, what I 'ad left over from yesterday and was warmin' up for 'im – when there comes a knock on my door. I goes and opens it, and there 'e was.

MINNIE. A policeman?

MRS MALTRAVERS. Plain clothes. Spotted who 'e was straight off. "Mrs Maltravers," he sez, and I sez, "That's right, and who might *you* be?" And he sez, "I'm a police orficer. Can I come in?" And I sez, "You'd better. I'm not standin' aht 'ere, I got a bit o' fish on the gas." So in 'is lordship comes, cool as a cucumber, and I sez, "You won't find no bettin' slips 'ere." And 'e sez, "Wot are yer talkin' abaht?" And *I* sez, "Ha!" – just like that. "Ha!" *(She chuckles.)* That put 'im back a bit.

MINNIE. Go on.

MRS MALTRAVERS. Then he draws aht a notebook and starts askin' me questions. All abaht these orfices. Was I the first 'ere this mornin', he wants to know. And I sez, "Yers, afore you was aht o' bed, I reckon." Then 'e sez, "'Ow did you get in?" And I sez, "Through the door. Think I come floatin' in the window like a bloomin' fairy?" Then 'e wants to know where I got the keys from. I tells 'im from Mr 'Arrison the porter. Then wot d'you think 'is nibs arsked?

MINNIE. I don't know.

MRS MALTRAVERS. Did I notice any footmarks on the floor?

MINNIE. Well?

MRS MALTRAVERS. "O' course not," I sez, "it's an *orfice*," I sez. "It was rainin' all day yesterday and abaht two 'undred people walked in an aht with their muddy boots. O' *course* there weren't no footmarks." I sez, "Wot d'yer think I'm hemployed for?" I asks 'im. "Ter clean the family jewels?" *(She chuckles.)* Oh, 'e didn't get much change aht o' *me*.

MINNIE. What did he say?

MRS MALTRAVERS. Starts to try and get shirty. "Remember I'm a police orficer," 'e sez, and, "That's easy," I sez. "Nobody other than a nark would ask such silly questions." Footmarks indeed.

NORAH. Then what happened, Mrs Maltravers?

MRS MALTRAVERS. Then 'e starts askin' questions abaht the safe in Mr McIntyre's orfice. And then 'e sez, "Did I see any blunt instrument lying around?" O' course, then I sees wot it's all abaht.

NORAH. What?

MRS MALTRAVERS. Murder, o' course. Don't you read the *News of the World?* When they starts talkin' abaht blunt instruments, it's always murder.

NORAH. Who murdered who?

MRS MALTRAVERS. That's wot 'is nibs wanted to find aht.

NORAH. *(With a touch of sarcasm.)* Did you tell him?

MRS MALTRAVERS. I did not. I don't 'old with police. Let them do their own dirty work.

(BEESLEY enters wearily up centre. MINNIE rises quickly, moves to her desk, and sits.)

BEESLEY. *(Taking off his hat and coat and hanging them on the pegs.)* What are *you* doing here, Mrs Maltravers?

MRS MALTRAVERS. *(Rising.)* Wot, *indeed.* I've come for a hexplanation – that's wot I've come for.

BEESLEY. *(Moving down centre.)* Concerning what?

MRS MALTRAVERS. Puttin' the police on to me. That nark said it was you who tole 'im where I lived.

(NORAH gives HEMMINGS a nudge, then sits at her desk. HEMMINGS sits up.)

BEESLEY. That is quite correct.

MRS MALTRAVERS. Well, I don't like it. See?

BEESLEY. Information was required from you regarding – a certain matter.

MRS MALTRAVERS. I consider it a liberty, Mr Beesley. I don't 'old with the police, and there's such a thing as declaration of character, I'd 'ave you know.

BEESLEY. *(Wearily.)* Don't be silly, Mrs Maltravers.

MRS MALTRAVERS. Silly, indeed. Why, while that chap was sittin' in my kitchen, Mr Maltravers came in, and it turned 'im all queer. Orf 'e goes agen like a rocket, and Gawd knows when I'll see 'im again. *And* 'e'd got a pass for two at the All-in Wrestlin' tonight.

BEESLEY. *(Testily.)* I really can't help that.

MRS MALTRAVERS. *Can't* yer? Well, we'll *see*. I'm goin' to 'ave it aht with Mr McIntyre.

BEESLEY. He's not here. He may not be back for a long time.

MRS MALTRAVERS. Then I'll 'ave it aht with 'im in the mornin'.

BEESLEY. No, you won't, because *you* won't be here in the morning.

MRS MALTRAVERS. What?

BEESLEY. Give me the petty cashbox. Miss Applin.

(**NORAH** *hands him the box.*)

(He takes some cash from the box.) Here you are, Mrs Maltravers. *(He holds out some cash.)* This takes you up till the end of the week.

MRS MALTRAVERS. Am I to understand that I'm bein' sacked?

BEESLEY. The firm will no longer be requiring your services.

MRS MALTRAVERS. You can't do this to *me*, Mr Beesley – that you can't.

BEESLEY. Nobody's doing anything to you. Take your money and go.

MRS MALTRAVERS. Ho! Indeed. Well, wot I say is...

BEESLEY. *(Firmly.)* Take your money and *go*.

> *(Something in his manner convinces* **MRS MALTRAVERS** *that argument is useless. She takes the cash and walks with dignity to the door up centre.)*

MRS MALTRAVERS. *(Turning.)* Now I know who did it.

BEESLEY. What?

MRS MALTRAVERS. The murder. *(She points dramatically at* **BEESLEY**.*)* You.

> *(She turns and exits.)*

BEESLEY. What the deuce is she talking about?

NORAH. She's got some silly idea in her head that someone has been killed.

BEESLEY. Killed?

NORAH. Murdered.

MINNIE. *(Timidly.)* Mr Beesley. Does it mean – paying her off like that – does it mean... *(She breaks off.)*

BEESLEY. Yes, Minnie. McIntyre and Blande is closing down – *definitely*.

MINNIE. *(Whispering.)* I see.

HEMMINGS. Surely the time has come when some explanation...

BEESLEY. Mr McIntyre will be back later. He's gone to see Mrs Blande. He may tell you all about it, or he may not. It's nothing to do with me.

*(**ELY** enters up centre. He looks very despondent. **BEESLEY** sits at his desk and begins to sort his letters, etc.)*

ELY. The return of the prodigal. *(He jerks his hat on to a peg.)* Behold the Good Samaritan. *(He stalks gloomily to his desk.)* Never, never again.

HEMMINGS. Never *what* again?

ELY. *(Sprawling in his chair.)* Never will I attempt to do anyone a good turn again. Julian Ely has learned his lesson. Never again.

HEMMINGS. What the devil are you talking about?

ELY. This afternoon I was gay – life was a bed of roses – now look at me. Portrait of a fool.

HEMMINGS. And a damn good one, too, but...

ELY. Take my advice, Hemmings, old boy. Never develop a conscience.

BEESLEY. Really, Ely – this is not the time for one of your silly jokes. Although the disaster which has overtaken the firm leaves you unaffected, you must remember that *others*...

ELY. That's the whole point, Ex-comrade Slave. I *did* remember the others. *(Headdresses all of them.)* As you may no doubt recollect, this afternoon certain comments were made in the office concerning the character of Julian Ely, and...

MINNIE. *(Protesting.)* You said we were to forget it.

ELY. No, Minnie – I said *you* were to forget it – that I would remember. And as Ely paced the unfriendly streets of the City of London, it dawned upon him that he was not perhaps the fine fellow he thought himself – in fact, that he was a bit of a snurge. So I said to myself, "How can I retrieve my unworthy past? How can Ely the stinker become Ely the hero, Ely the saviour of his side?"

HEMMINGS. How?

ELY. Allow me to tell my tragic story my own way, my noble Hemmings. After much cogitation an idea struck me, and after I had picked myself up from the pavement and dusted my clothes, I hailed a taxi and proceeded to the office of my Guv'nor – Ely the First of Great Renown. There I recounted what had befallen the firm of McIntyre and Blande, and said, "Poppa, dear – this has knocked some of my poor comrades flat – you have branches and offices, and *you* shall employ them."

MINNIE. Oh, Mr Ely – how kind of you.

ELY. Wait, wait. This is a tragic story – it has no happy ending.

MINNIE. You mean…?

ELY. My stern parent said, "Nothing doing, my son. I am fully staffed and considering reductions. Sorry I am to hear of these misfortunes, but I can do naught to assist."

MINNIE. Oh! Still, all the same…

ELY. *(Sweeping on.)* But *that* is not the worst. Horror upon horror's head accumulatesm – as Hemmings would say. "The only person I *can* put into a job", said my noble sire, "is *you.*" Me. I ask you? "How fortunate you've come in this afternoon," he continued, "my friend Billington wants someone for his Manchester office, and I'll fix you there." *Manchester* of all places.

HEMMINGS. Bad luck, old boy.

ELY. No, damn bad generalship. Don't you see? If only I'd kept my silly mouth shut for a day or two, the damned vacancy would have been filled. *Now,* what's happened – goodbye to Piccadilly, farewell to Leicester

Square. Poor Ely is to be banished to the dank mists of Manchester.

HEMMINGS. Well, it's a funny world – the only chap who doesn't need a job, gets one.

ELY. This crib was bad enough, but it *did* have it's lighter side – the comic capers of the excellent Beesley, for instance, but – *Manchester*. Well, Ely has learned his lesson. When – as will probably soon happen – he has died in the sunless North of a broken heart, let this inscription mark his grave. "His first good deed was his last."

BEESLEY. Well, Ely, the episode doesn't seem to have ended as you hoped for, but at the same time, I think your companions should thank you for…

*(**BOBBIE DRUCE**, excitedly reading an evening paper, burst in up centre.)*

Well, really.

BOBBIE. Here, I say. Look at this. All about Mr Blande.

BEESLEY. *(Rising.)* What?

BOBBIE. *(Spreading the paper over the desk centre, right of **NORAH**.)* Look at this. *(He reads.)* "Dramatic scene at Folkestone."

*(**MINNIE** rises and leans over **BOBBIE**'s right shoulder, **HEMMINGS** and **NORAH** lean across the desk from their seats, **ELY** rises, moves and leans over **BOBBIE**'s left shoulder.)*

"Man killed by paddle – which… believed to be Arthur Blande, well known in the City… Police pursuit ends in tragedy… missing securities."

HEMMINGS. Crikey!

*(They all look at **BEESLEY**.)*

So *that's* what it's all about.

BEESLEY. *(Slowly.)* Yes. I had no idea it would get in the papers tonight.

BOBBIE. This is the Late Final. One of our chaps wanted it for the result of the four o'clock.

MINNIE. Poor Mr. Blande!

BEESLEY. Poor Mr *McIntyre*!

HEMMINGS. Poor *us*!

ELY. *(Easing down left.)* Do you really mean to say that Mr Blande has robbed the firm?

BEESLEY. Yes. There's no point in concealing the information now that it has reached the press. Last night, some valuable securities were deposited here, and placed in the safe in Mr McIntyre's room. Apparently overcome by temptation, Mr Blande returned and absconded with them. The police were informed and – *(He indicates the paper.)* – the rest is there.

NORAH. And Mr McIntyre...?

BEESLEY. Is unable to meet his commitments. He's a ruined man.

ELY. I'll be damned! And people say City life is dull.

> *(**MCINTYRE** enters up centre. **MINNIE** moves quickly to her desk. There is a few moments silence as **MCINTYRE** surveys them.)*

MCINTYRE. *(To **BOBBIE**.)* Yes – what do you want?

BOBBIE. Nothing, sir – I – nothing, sir.

> *(He exits up centre.)*

BEESLEY. *(Moving to the desk centre and picking up the newspaper.)* Have you seen the evening paper, sir? *(He hands **MCINTYRE** the paper.)*

MCINTYRE. No. *(He takes the paper and reads.)* Oh! *(He puts the paper on the desk, takes off his hat, moves and hangs it on the pegs.)* You'd better all sit down.

*(***BEESLEY*** sits in the chair down centre, **ELY** and **MINNIE** sit at their desks.)*

(He moves right of the desk centre.) Well, I suppose you all know what all the trouble has been about. What isn't in the paper, I expect Beesley has explained to you. *(He glances at **BEESLEY**.)*

*(**BEESLEY** nods.)*

I don't intend to make a speech, but there are just one or two things I *must* say. When I spoke to you this afternoon, I had a faint hope that the – er – disaster which threatened the firm might be averted. I'm sorry to say that hope has now gone. A man I regarded as a loyal partner and my best friend, has robbed me. A swift and terrible retribution has overtaken him, but unfortunately, it makes no difference to the firm. The securities with which he decamped have not been recovered, and there is no hope now that they *will* be. Either he disposed of them before he tried to escape to the Continent, or they were destroyed at the time of his death. The only point that really concerns me, is that I am responsible for them. The firm of McIntyre and Blande is finished.

(There are murmurs of sympathy.)

I assure you that if there was the slightest possibility of carrying on, I would do so, but – I don't want to be melodramatic – I am a ruined man. As you can well imagine, I'm feeling pretty sorry for myself, but I should like to repeat what I said this afternoon – I'm deeply sorry for you too. I quite realize that to be suddenly thrown out of employment like this, will hit some of you very hard indeed. Today is Tuesday.

There will be a certain amount of work to be done, clearing up the affairs of the office, but I think all that can be concluded by Friday. Leave of absence for any of you who require time off to seek employment will be granted, and on Friday, everyone will receive a fortnight's salary in lieu of notice. And I should like to express my deep appreciation of your good service and loyalty to me in the past. That is all. *(He turns to move into the inner office.)*

BEESLEY. *(Rising.)* Excuse me one moment, sir. On behalf of the members of the firm, I should like to express…

> *(There is a sudden commotion, with shouting, off stage up centre.)*

MCINTYRE. *(Moving to the door up centre and opening it.)* What the devil?

BOBBIE. *(Off; shouting.)* I've got him. Help, help. I've got him.

> *(***BOBBIE DRUCE** *and* **ARTHUR BLANDE**, *struggling desperately, reel in up centre.* **ARTHUR BLANDE** *is in the middle forties. He has been carrying a bunch of tulips, and as they struggle, the almost dead flowers are scattered about the floor.* **BOBBIE** *is bleeding from the nose and his collar is torn. Everyone rises.)*

Help! Lend a hand. I've got him!

BLANDE. *(Breaking away.)* You young devil!

BOBBIE. No, you don't. *(He closes with* **BLANDE** *again and plants a blow on his chin.* **BLANDE** *falls to the floor right of the desk centre, knocked out.)* Hold that, you blighter.

HEMMING. It's Blande! Good heavens! Mr Blande!

MCINTYRE. What on earth?

MINNIE. *(Moving in left of* **BOBBIE.***)* Bobbie, are you hurt?

(**BEESLEY** *kneels beside* **BLANDE.***)*

BOBBIE. *(Breathlessly.)* No, I'm all right. Crumbs, he's tough, though. I had a heli of a job getting him up those stairs.

MCINTYRE. *(To* **BEESLEY.***)* Is he all right?

BEESLEY. Yes, I think so, sir.

MCINTYRE. Get him into a chair.

(**HEMMINGS** *assists* **BEESLEY** *to lift* **BLANDE** *into the chair down centre, then moves left of the desk centre.* **BEESLEY** *stands right of* **BLANDE.***)*

ELY. Gratters, young Druce – a pretty paste that – a very pretty paste.

NORAH. *(Moving to the door up centre.)* I'll get some water.

MCINTYRE. Yes, Miss Applin.

(**NORAH** *exits up centre.*)

MINNIE. Oh, Bobbie, your nose is bleeding something awful.

BOBBIE. *(The hero of the hour.)* Is it? Well, never mind about that. I got the blighter. *(To* **MCINTYRE.***)* I was just nipping out of our office to post the mail, sir, when I saw him in the main doorway. "No time to lose", I thought, and I went straight at him, hell for leather. *Did* he struggle, sir? I'll say he did – not half strong.

MCINTYRE. He played rugger for Richmond years ago.

BOBBIE. I had *my* work cut out, and no mistake. Of course, he's *heavier* than me.

> (**NORAH** *enters up centre carrying a glass of water. She gives it to* **BEESLEY**, *then moves to her seat and sits.* **MCINTYRE** *is centre.* **ELY** *crosses left of* **BLANDE**. **HEMMINGS** *is by the window up left.* **MINNIE**, *up centre, takes her handkerchief from her handbag and tries to clean* **BOBBIE**'s *face. He is right of her.*)

MINNIE. Bobbie, you're a hero.

BOBBIE. Oh, shut up, Min.

ELY. If you've saved me from Manchester, young Druce, I'll stand you a supper at the Troc.

MINNIE. He's saved us *all*.

> (**BEESLEY** *splashes some water in* **BLANDE**'s *face.*)

MCINTYRE. That remains to be seen. It depends what he's done with those bonds.

> (**BLANDE** *stirs.*)

BEESLEY. I think he's coming round, sir.

> (*There is a pause. They all stare at* **BLANDE** *as he sits up in the chair, and puts a hand to the back of his neck, where, as is usual, the knock-out on the point of his chin has caused a shock to his spine at the base of his skull. He gazes round with glassy eyes.* **BEESLEY** *puts the glass on the table right centre.*)

BLANDE. What the devil… (*He sees* **BOBBIE**.) You young… (*He tries to rise.*)

ELY. (*Moving behind* **BLANDE** *and pulling him back into the chair.*) No, you don't!

BLANDE. (*Recovering quickly.*) Let me get at him. I'll teach him. Let go my arms, damn you!

ELY. *(Gripping* **BLANDE** *still tighter.)* Steady the Buffs.

BLANDE. *(Furiously.)* Will – you – let go. *(To* **MCINTYRE.***)* Don't stand there staring, you fool. Send for the police.

MCINTYRE. The police!

(There is general amazement.)

BLANDE. Yes, the police, or someone with a strait-jacket. *(He nods at* **BOBBIE.***)* If you let him get away...

MCINTYRE. *(Moving left of* **BLANDE.***)* He won't get away. Neither will *you*, Blande. *Where are those bonds?*

BLANDE. What bonds?

MCINTYRE. *(Very sternly.)* You know perfectly well what I'm talking about. Those securities Mrs Winterstone brought in last night.

BLANDE. Those?

MCINTYRE. Yes. Are you going to deny you took them out of my safe?

BLANDE. Of course I took them out.

MCINTYRE. Then where are they? Answer me. Where are they?

BLANDE. Where are they? In the bank, of course.

MCINTYRE. *What* bank?

BLANDE. My bank – your bank – *our* bank, you damn fool!

(There is a pause.)

MCINTYRE. You mean – you didn't – you haven't...

BLANDE. Haven't what? Don't ask me silly questions. Ring up the police and get that young blackguard arrested. Assault and battery, that's what it is. Unprovoked assault. I'll teach him!

MCINTYRE. Steady on, Blande. I think there's been a bit of a mistake.

BLANDE. There'll be no mistake when I get my hands on him. If a man can't walk peacefully into his own office without being man-handled by a young thug who...

MCINTYRE. Now, now – take it easy. What I want to know is this – are those securities safe?

BLANDE. Unless the bank's been robbed. I tell you they're in the bank.

MCINTYRE. Where's that paper?

NORAH. Here you are, sir. *(She picks up the newspaper from the desk and hands it to* **MCINTYRE**.*)*

MCINTYRE. *(Holding out the paper to* **BLANDE**.*)* You'd better read this.

*(***ELY*** releases ***BLANDE***'s arms, and joins ***HEMMINGS*** by the window left.)*

BLANDE. Why? *(He takes the paper and reads.)* "Dramatic scene at Folkestone... Arthur Blande...police." *(He rubs his eyes.)* My head's singing like hell. What *is* this – some damn fool joke?

MCINTYRE. No joke, old boy. We thought you were dead.

BLANDE. Me, dead? *(He re-reads the paragraph.)* "Wanted man... Missing securities?" Hell's bells. I'll have them for libel. Get the editor. Ring my solicitors. *(Suddenly.)* What *started* this damn fool nonsense?

MCINTYRE. Well, you see... *(He hesitates.)*

BLANDE. Don't tell me you had anything to do with it. If so, I'll *have you* for slander. I'll dissolve partnership. I'll...

MCINTYRE. Go easy, old boy.

BLANDE. Easy! Look at the way I've been treated. Heaven knows, I was feeling ill enough before any of this happened. All this in the paper – a sock in the jaw from that young hooligan, and...

MCINTYRE. Would you like a spot of whisky, old boy?

BLANDE. Ugh! Don't you mention whisky to me. Give me a cup of tea.

MCINTYRE. Minnie.

> (**MINNIE** *moves to the door up centre and exits.*)

Now, old man, don't you think you'd better explain?

BLANDE. *(Angrily.)* Me? *Me* explain. *(He waves the paper.)* You have the infernal impertinence to blacken my character, set the police after me, throw me under a paddle wheel at Folkestone harbour, and then ask me to explain.

MCINTYRE. You *must* see how it all happened. After all, we found the safe had been tampered with, the securities had gone. *You* were missing, and your wife said...

BLANDE. Does *she* know anything about this?

MCINTYRE. Well, you see...

BLANDE. The rate you've all been moving, I expect she's drawn my life insurance by now.

MCINTYRE. Beesley. Get on to Mrs Blande at once – there's a line through in Mr Blande's office.

BEESLEY. Yes, sir.

> (*He hurries to the door up centre, nearly colliding with* **MINNIE** *who enters with a cup of tea.*)

Really, Minnie! *Do* be careful.

(He exits up centre. **MINNIE** *moves right of* **BLANDE**.*)*

BLANDE. Where's that tea?

*(****MINNIE*** *takes the newspaper from him, and hands him the cup.)*

Thank you, Minnie. *(He drinks.)* Talk about a head...

*(****MINNIE*** *places the paper on the table right centre.)*

BOBBIE. I'm awfully sorry, Mr Blande.

BLANDE. I should think you are. *(He puts his tongue out suddenly at* **MCINTYRE**.*)* Look at my tongue.

MCINTYRE. *(Recoiling.)* My dear chap...

BLANDE. Now you know the state of my liver. *(He finishes the tea.)* That's better. *(He hands the cup to* **MINNIE**.*)*

*(****MINNIE*** *takes the cup and joins* **BOBBIE** *up centre. She puts the cup on her desk.)*

MCINTYRE. Then I do think you might tell us where you've been. After all, there has been a certain confusion in the office today, and...

BLANDE. It all started last night. You remember Mrs Winterstone brought in those securities, and I pointed out that they were all negotiable, and anyone could push off with them?

MCINTYRE. Yes, yes, of course.

BLANDE. You locked them in the safe, and we went over the road and had a drink. Then you went off home and left me waiting for my bus.

MCINTYRE. Yes, go on.

BLANDE. Well, the first damn bus was full, and I had to wait for another. I was standing there, when, with no warning at all, a chap came up behind me and snatched my brief case. Naturally, I chased after him, but he had the legs of me, and slipped off into some side alley. Of course, I was damned angry, but there was nothing of value in the case, so I decided it wasn't worth trying to catch him. I was late, not too popular at home, and the whole thing could be dealt with in the morning. So back I came to the bus stop, just in time to miss *another* one. Well, as I stood there cussing and blinding, a thought went through my mind, "This is a nice thing," I thought, "bag-snatching in the streets of the City – talk about a crime wave." And then I remembered those bonds. "Suppose someone should break into the office," I thought, "and that fool hasn't locked the safe properly."

MCINTYRE. What fool?

BLANDE. You. So I decided the best thing to do was to come back and see.

MCINTYRE. And *was* it locked?

BLANDE. It was. But, for some reason or other – I don't know what, I opened it, saw the bonds were safely there, and then... *(He shrugs his shoulders.)*

MCINTYRE. What?

BLANDE. The infernal thing wouldn't shut again. Something had gone wrong with the lock. I got my knife and tinkered about with it, but it was no good. So there I was.

MCINTYRE. Yes. What did you do?

BLANDE. Well, I most certainly wasn't going to leave them like that. Neither was I going to take them home with me, after my other pleasant little experience. So I did them up in a parcel, and trotted over to the bank with them. I knew there'd be a night watchman or someone, but as luck would have it, one of the cashiers was still there, working late. He took them, and said he'd bang them into the strong room. Then, back I went again, and of course I missed *another* bus. By that time I was fed to the teeth, so I went into the *Crown* again, to have a drink. And there, leaning against the bar, was old Charlie Peterson.

MCINTYRE. Who the devil's he?

BLANDE. Charlie Peterson? Why, the old English rugger captain, of course. We were in the Richmond team together, before he retired and went to South Africa. Hadn't seen him for over ten years. He's just landed, and was on his way north – catching the night Scot from Euston. Well, as you can imagine, we had a snifter to celebrate seeing each other again. Then we had another, and another, and I kept meaning to ring up my wife, and then kept forgetting to do so. And then he said he wanted a meal, so we turned into Blair's Chop House, and had a meal. Then we had a few more drinks, and drifted down to the West End. I remembered a little club in Soho I used to go to, and we went off there, and *then*...

MCINTYRE. What?

BLANDE. I suppose I must have passed out. I'm not used to these binges these days. The next thing I remember, I was in bed at the Grand Palace Hotel. It was half-past four in the afternoon, and I felt like a seasick polecat.

MCINTYRE. How did you get there?

BLANDE. Good old Charlie. He left a note explaining. He simply *had* to catch his night train, had no idea where I lived, and parked me there to sleep it off. So I got up, paid the bill, came along here in a taxi, and – *(He shakes his fat at* **BOBBIE**.*)* – that young gorilla sprang at me in the hall, tore my coat, tried to strangle me, and then knocked me out with a lucky one.

MCINTYRE. Extraordinary. All I can say is, "All's well that ends well."

BLANDE. Hell to that! What's *well* about it?

(**BEESLEY** *enters up centre.*)

(To **BEESLEY**.*)* Did you get on to my wife?

BEESLEY. *(Moving right of* **BLANDE**.*)* Yes, Mr Blande. Everything's all right, and...

BLANDE. Sez you. *(To* **MCINTYRE**.*)* I'm not explaining any more. Shall need all that when I get home. *(He rises.)* Crikey, what a head!

MCINTYRE. *(Taking* **BLANDE**'s *arm.)* Come and sit down quietly in your room.

BLANDE. *(Putting a hand to his head).* Yes, I think I will.

(**MCINTYRE** *leads* **BLANDE** *to the door up centre.)*

BOBBIE. *(Stepping forward.)* Really, Mr Blande – I'm terribly sorry.

BLANDE. *(Fiercely.)* I should damn well think you *are*. You play for some silly soccer team, don't you?

BOBBIE. Yes, sir.

BLANDE. Take up rugger. You're *wasted,* my lad!

(**MCINTYRE** *and* **BLANDE** *exit up centre.)*

BOBBIE. *(Turning and moving in to* **MINNIE**.*)* Did you hear that? I don't think he'll get me sacked after all. Everything's all right.

MINNIE. Darling. *(She embraces and kisses him.)*

ELY. Oi, oi, oi! Break away there! *(He seizes* **HEMMINGS** *and starts to waltz him round.)* Saved, by gosh! Saved from a fate worse than death in Manchester. *(He stops* *and looks up at the clock.)* They're open. Come on. I'll buy you a quart.

BEESLEY. Once and for all, I cannot allow...

ELY. *(Propelling* **HEMMINGS** *to the door up centre.)* Pipe down Comrade Slave. The night is young and throats are dry.

*(***HEMMINGS** *and* **ELY** *exit up centre.)*

BEESLEY. Really. In all my experience I never – well!

BOBBIE. *(Moving to the door up centre.)* I must get off downstairs. They'll wonder what's happened to me. So long, Min – see you later.

(He exits up centre. **MCINTYRE** *enters up centre.* **MINNIE** *sits at her desk.)*

MCINTYRE. Oh, I say, Beesley – where are Ely and Hemmings?

BEESLEY. They've... I told them they could go, sir.

MCINTYRE. Oh, did you? Well, never mind. But there's a devil of a lot to be done. We haven't done a stroke of work in the office all day, and there are a lot of letters to get off. I don't want to impose on anyone, but I wonder if you'd mind staying late? What about you, Miss Applin?

NORAH. Well – I ... *(She hesitates.)* Certainly, Mr McIntyre.

MCINTYRE. Thanks. Find the carbon of that letter to Tomlinsons, will you? And Beesley, I shall want the Fitz-Patrick file. *(He moves into the inner office, sits, and starts to sort the letters on his desk.)*

*(***NORAH** *looks through her papers for the copy letter.* **BEESLEY** *moves to the cupboard up left and looks for the fie. The telephone rings and* **MINNIE** *lifts the receiver.)*

MINNIE. *(Speaking into the telephone.)* McIntyre and Blande... Hold on, please. *(She turns to **NORAH**, covering the receiver with her hand.)* It's for you, Miss Applin.

NORAH. *(Tensely.)* Who is it?

MINNIE. It's from a call-box. I heard the pennies drop. Then I heard a train whistle, too. I think it's from a station.

NORAH. Say – say I've gone home.

MINNIE. You mean...?

NORAH. Say I've gone home.

MINNIE. OK. *(Into the telephone.)* I'm sorry, but Miss Applin has gone – home. *(She replaces the receiver.)* Then...

NORAH. *(Quietly.)* It's all right, Minnie.

MINNIE. Oh, I say, isn't life wonderful?

*(**BLANDE** enters up centre.)*

BLANDE. Has anyone seen any flowers?

BEESLEY. *(Moving centre.)* Flowers, sir?

BLANDE. Yes, the ones I was taking home to my wife.

*(**BEESLEY** looks around and then points to the scattered ruins of the tulips on the floor. They both stare at them as – .)*

(The curtain falls.)

FURNITURE AND PROPERTY LIST

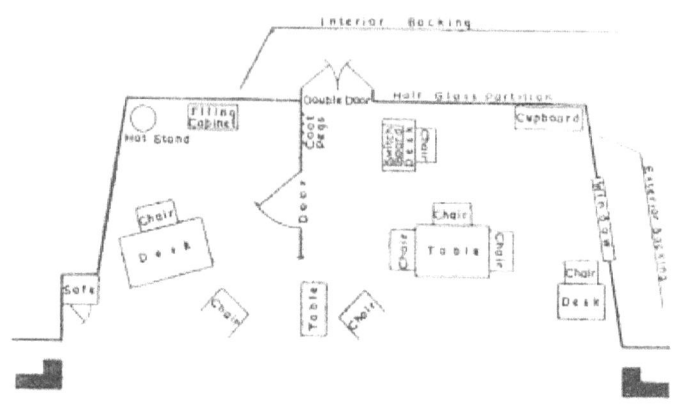

Throughout the play:

On stage:
>Desk (McIntyre). *On it:* blotter, inkstand, pens, telephone, 2 letter baskets, ashtray, letters and papers.
>
>Safe. *In it:* documents.
>
>Filing cabinet.
>
>Hat stand.
>
>Waste-paper basket (*Inner office*).
>
>2 chairs (*Inner office*).
>
>Large desk. *On it right;* dirty blotting-paper, inkwell, pens, ashtray, letter basket, folders, letters and paper, memo pad.
>
>*On it centre:* blotter, inkwell, pens, documents, letter basket, petty cashbox containing cash.
>
>*On it left*: blotter, inkwell, pens, documents, ledger.
>
>Desk (Ely). *On it:* blotter, inkwell, pens, letter basket, documents.
>
>6 chairs (*Outer office*).
>
>Table (*Right centre*). *On it:* ledgers, typewriters.
>
>Cupboard (*Up left*). *In it:* clean blotting-paper, files.
>
>Desk (Minnie). *On it:* telephone switchboard, papers.

Carpet on the floor (*Inner office only*).
Waste-paper basket (*Above desk centre, outer office*).
Clock (*Over window left*).

ACT ONE

Set in inner office:
Dustpan.
Brush.
Mop.

Personal:
MRS MALTRAVERS: Duster.
MINNIE: Attaché-case. *In it:* magazine.
Handbag. *In it:* powder compact, handkerchief.
NORAH: Handbag. *In it:* powder compact, handkerchief.
BEESLEY: Pince-nez, umbrella, brief-case, 2 railway tickets.
MCINTYRE: Watch, keys.
ALICE: Handbag.
RUPERT: Spectacles.
MRS BLANDE: Handbag. *In it:* hankerchief.

ACT TWO

Collect documents off inner office floor and replace them in safe. Reset clock.
Strike from pegs: Hat and coat (Hemmings).
Hat and coat (Norah).
Hat and coat (Minnie).
Hat (Ely).

Offstage:
  Office papers (McIntyre).

Personal:
  MCINTYRE: Cigarette lighter, cigarette-case. *In it:* 2 cigarettes only.
  BEESLEY: One shilling and tenpence in cash.
  HEMMINGS: Newspaper.

ACT THREE

Strike from pegs:
  Hat and coat (Beesley).

Strike from the hatstand:
  Hat (McIntyre).
  Reset clock.

Set:

Dirty teacups { 1 (Minnie).
1 (Norah).
1 (Hemmings). }

Offstage:
  Cup of tea for Mrs Maltravers (Minnie).
  Cup of tea for Mr Blande (Minnie).
  Glass of water (Norah).
  Evening paper (Bobbie).
  Bunch of tulips (Blande).

www.ingramcontent.com/pod-product-compliance
Ingram Content Group UK Ltd.
Pitfield, Milton Keynes, MK11 3LW, UK
UKHW021839210426
5322IPUK00022B/375